D0819474

MOVIE TRIVIA
MADNESS

INTERESTING FACTS AND TRIVIA

BEST TRIVIA BOOKS VOL.1

BY
BILL O'NEILL & STEVE MURRAY

ISBN-13: 978-1544739274

DON'T FORGET YOUR FREE BOOKS

CONTENTS

Introduction.. 1

CHAPTER ONE: THE MOVIE STARS 3

Leonardo DiCaprio.. 3

Daniel Day-Lewis.. 4

Jack Nicholson 5

Jim Carrey 5

Natalie Portman... 6

Bill Murray 6

Jennifer Lawrence 7

Anthony Hopkins 8

Arnold Schwarzenegger 8

Christian Bale 9

Robert Downey Jr... 9

Robin Williams.. 10

Will Smith 11

Nicole Kidman 12

Heath Ledger 12

Random Fun Facts.. 14

Test Yourself - Questions And Answers 18

CHAPTER TWO : Lights...Camera...ACTION!................ 20

    Pirates of the Caribbean 20

    Fight Club 21

    Indiana Jones... 22

    300.. 23

    Die Hard... 23

    Saving Private Ryan 24

    X-Men 25

    Rocky 25

    Charlie and the Chocolate Factory 27

    Catch Me If You Can.. 27

    Terminator 2: Judgement Day 28

    Superman 29

    Ong-bak: The Thai Warrior 30

    Forrest Gump 30

    Guardians of the Galaxy....................................... 31

  Random Fun Facts 33

    Test Yourself - Questions And Answers 37

CHAPTER THREE: Science Fiction & Fantasy 39

    The Lord of the Rings 39

    Harry Potter... 41

    Star Wars 41

    Avatar 42

Wizard of Oz 43

Star Trek 43

2001: A Space Odyssey 44

Fifth Element 45

Creatures Come to Life 46

Robots Come to Life 46

Hunger Games 47

Planet of the Apes 48

Pan's Labyrinth 48

The Princess Bride 49

E.T. 50

Random Fun Facts 51

Test Yourself - Questions And Answers 55

CHAPTER FOUR: The Director's Cut 58

The Legend 58

The Visionaries 59

An American Icon 60

The Perfectionist 61

Devoted Craftsmen 61

The Maestro 62

The Rebel 63

Passion Project! 65

Creating a Masterpiece 65

The Neurotic Genius 66

Family Man 67

From Monty Python to 12 Monkeys...via Brazil................ 69

A New Kind of Pitch 70

The Eccentric 70

The Mythical and the Mysterious....................................... 71

Random Fun Facts 73

Test Yourself - Questions And Answers 77

CHAPTER FIVE: Anything For A Laugh **79**

The Frat Pack 79

The Big Lebowski 80

The Hangover.. 81

A Green Ogre and a Donkey 81

He Fooled You... 82

Shaun of the Dead 83

Clerks 84

Team America World Police are.....puppets?...................... 84

Wayne's World... 86

Forgetting Sarah Marshall... 86

Snatch... 87

Fear and Loathing in Las Vegas 88

Jim Carrey 88

Adam Sandler and Co 89

Austin Powers... 90

Random Fun Facts.. 91

Test Yourself - Questions And Answers 95

CHAPTER SIX: Things Take A Dramatic Turn............... 97

Gangs of New York 97

The Wolf of Wall Street... 98

Eyes Wide Shut 99

The Deer Hunter... 100

The Truman Show 101

The Curious Case of Benjamin Button.............................. 102

No Country For Old Men 103

The People vs. Larry Flint... 104

Apocalypto 104

12 Years A Slave.. 105

Boyhood 106

There Will Be Blood... 107

Fury 107

Castaway 108

Random Fun Facts... 110

Test Yourself - Questions And Answers 114

CHAPTER SEVEN: BITS & BITES..............................117

What's With The Teeth?... 117

Method Acting Madness... 118

Strange Inspiration 120

Costumes So Good They Hurt 121

Before They Were Famous.. 122

Quiet On The Set! 122

What Are They Smoking? 123

Tinsel Town.. 124

Doing Honour to Improv.. 125

Danger on Set... 125

What Do They Do With All That Money? 126

Off Camera Antics.. 127

Strange Diets 128

Lying To Get The Part.. 129

What's That Sound?.. 130

Random Fun Facts 132

Test Yourself - Questions And Answers 136

INTRODUCTION

Are you ready to learn all the interesting and fun facts from your favourite movies? Because if you're a big movie fan, then this is the perfect book for you. It's chock full of all the details that you probably never knew about. You get to go behind the scenes and get all the crazy stories from the sets of the movies you love. You'll find out what motivates and inspires Hollywood's A-list actors and how they prepare for their biggest roles. You'll see how some directors have had to struggle and innovate to get their projects to the screen, and learn the secrets behind some of the more interesting movie effects around.

This book won't just entertain you, it'll enrich your movie watching experience. You'll look at the craft of acting in a new light and notice details in films that you never saw before. For example, did you know that a couple of Star Wars characters make a rather unique cameo in one of the Indiana Jones movies? You'll also probably get a new respect for film makers and what they sometimes have to endure to make sure you the fan are getting to watch the best possible version of their vision. One director even had to hold secret screenings of his banned film to force the studio to finally release it!

In these pages, you'll learn things you never knew about your favourite actors and actresses. You'll find out which actress has a virtual zoo of taxidermy animals in her apartment, and which mega-star actor still collects Barbie Dolls! You'll learn which of your favourite scenes were total accidents and completely improvised, but ended up being some of the best parts of the film. Can you guess which movie had the sound department rubbing pumpkins together and then recording it to use as an alien language? All this and much, much more. We dug deep to get only the most interesting facts for you to enjoy. There's over 400 of them from all of your favourite flicks!

So settle in and enjoy the ride. The book is broken into seven easy to read chapters. And each one comes with a section of fun and challenging trivia questions for you to test your movie knowledge with! You'll go on a journey that takes you through the jokes from the kings of comedy, to some of the most powerful dramatic roles on screen. You'll take a trip through the world of science fiction and learn which actress actually invented a new language for her performance. And you won't believe what some actors have had to endure just to get into costume for their roles. And all for the love of film!

That's right, this is THE book for movie fans. How do we know? Because we love movies too!

So please enjoy this collection of random, interesting, fun and entertaining movie trivia!

CHAPTER ONE

THE MOVIE STARS

Actors are the storytellers of our time. They are craftsmen in the art of film, and have brought to life untold remarkable characters for us to enjoy. But underneath all the fame and celebrity, they are often just like the people who watch them onscreen. They make mistakes, and they sometimes have strange behaviours. More often, they're as interested in movie making as us fans. So enjoy these interesting facts from some of your favourite Hollywood icons.

LEONARDO DICAPRIO

Leonardo DiCaprio is quite the grandiose name. And while many actors have been known to take a 'stage name' when they start their careers, Leo's came to him naturally. As the story goes, baby Leo started kicking inside his pregnant mom while his parents were looking at a Da Vinci painting on their honeymoon in Italy. His father took it as a sign and named him on the spot.

As a child actor, Leo ignored his agent's advice to change his name to the Americanized, "Lenny Williams", and in fact copyrighted his own name in 1999. Morgan Freeman followed suit and trademarked his name as well. Needless to say, I think we're all glad Leo stayed unique and kept his original name.

The girls are certainly happy for his rise to fame. Apparently 7% of teenage girls in America had watched 'Titanic' twice within the first five weeks of its release!

DANIEL DAY-LEWIS

He has a method! Acclaimed Irish actor Daniel Day-Lewis is well known for immersing himself completely into his roles. Sometimes to the detriment of his own health. In fact, he caught pneumonia during the filming of 'Gangs of New York', because he refused to wear any clothing that didn't keep with the time period. No warm jackets for Bob the Butcher.

Daniel spent two months preparing for his role in 'The Age of Innocence' by walking around New York City in a top hat and cane. And for 'Last of the Mohicans', he spent months living in the forest, learning how to track, hunt and skin animals, and only ate food he caught himself.

His character in 'My Left Foot' was bound to a wheelchair, so he never left his chair either. This meant the staff had to lift him around set and spoon feed him his meals. For the filming of, 'In the Name of the Father', he spent his nights locked in solitary confinement in an abandoned prison. Crew members threw water and insults at him and he lost 30 pounds! For the 'Crucible'? He decided not to bathe, of course, to get the feel for 17th century living standards. I'm sure the crew liked that one!

JACK NICHOLSON

Want to know how to agitate Jack Nicholson? Well, apparently, he hates cheese sandwiches. So Stanley Kubrick, director of the 'Shining', made sure that was all that was available to his star actor. He wanted to ensure he was in the right mood to play a man going insane!

Or you could do what Hunter S. Thompson did. As a prank on Jack's birthday, Hunter shone a massive spotlight on his house, while blasting a gruesome recording of a pig being eaten alive by bears. Hunter topped it off by firing his pistol, and left a freshly-cut elk's heart on Jack's front door. All this going on while Nicholson and his two daughters hid for their safety in the basement!

JIM CARREY

You just can't contain a guy like Jim! Many of his best scenes are improvised and memorable lines are often completely spontaneous. Remember the "most annoying sound in the world" from 'Dumb and Dumber'? You could probably tell this wasn't in the script by the genuinely horrified look on Jeff Daniel's face as Jim leans over and lets him hear it. It was off the cuff in typical Carrey style. And in the bar scene in Aspen, the line "No way... that's great. We've landed on the moon!" was also made up by Jim right on the spot when he saw the framed newspaper.

Some say Jim hasn't taken any dramatic roles lately due to poor box office performance of his previous ones. But apparently, he will only perform in a movie that has a completely positive message. He has struggled with depression, and due to his own personal belief system doesn't want to project anything negative.

NATALIE PORTMAN

Dedicated to her craft. The budget for 'Black Swan' was apparently so tight that the production couldn't afford to have a medic on site. Natalie Portman learned of this after she badly dislocated a rib. In order to get the funds for a medic, she said they could take away her trailer. Which they did!

Natalie was entirely devoted to the project, and trained for an entire year to prepare for the role as lead ballerina. Not only that, she paid for the training herself until investors were found to fund the project. On top of her preparation for 'Black Swan', she lost 20 pounds for the role, which is a lot for a girl that only weighs 115 pounds!

And for 'V for Vendetta', she worked with a voice coach to perfect an English accent, and readily looked forward to having her head completely shaved on film. They got it in one take. They had to!

BILL MURRAY

Immortalized! Plenty of actors get their hand and foot prints memorialized on Hollywood Boulevard, but Bill Murray has a distinct claim of his own. A plaque marks the spot in Woodstock, Illinois where he repeatedly stepped in a puddle for the movie 'Groundhog Day'. Yes, oddities seem to surround the famous and reclusive actor.

In fact, Bill doesn't even have a publicist. Nor an agent. In 1999, he replaced his agency with an automated voice mailbox that can only be reached by an 800 number that he gives out rather rarely. The best you can do is leave a message and hope he gets back to you. Which is what Sofia Coppola did. After leaving hundreds of messages to get Bill to star in her movie 'Lost In Translation', he finally called her back to discuss the role. But she was never sure he would actually show up for the film until he was there in person. All they had was a verbal confirmation. Bill was true to his word.

JENNIFER LAWRENCE

A self-described tomboy growing up, Jennifer wasn't allowed to play with other girls in preschool. Apparently, she was "too rough". Her co-star in the 'Hunger Games', Josh Hutcherson found that one out the hard way. Apparently, while goofing around, she actually knocked him out with a head kick and gave him a concussion!

But her tough streak didn't stop her from being discovered by Hollywood. And 'discovered' is exactly what happened. Her big break came when she was in New York on spring break with her family. She was approached in the street by an agent, had her picture taken, and was called the next day to do a screen test. The rest is history, as they say.

Voted most talkative by her class mates, Lawrence has gone on to perform many acclaimed roles....and hilarious interviews. Check them out online if you haven't seen them already. Talkative indeed!

ANTHONY HOPKINS

They never even met! Apparently co-stars Jodie Foster and Anthony Hopkins never spoke to each other out of character on the set of 'Silence of the Lambs'. The two were always separated by glass partitions, and Anthony was often in shackles and mask.

According to Jodie, she avoided Hopkins. As she puts it, "He was too scary!" Maybe it was the unusual touches he used for his character development of Hannibal Lecter. He purposefully used a cutting tone of voice, and never blinked. He picked this particularly unnerving trait up after watching film of convicted murderer Charles Manson. His disturbing slurping sounds after describing a gruesome act of cannibalism probably didn't help either. All improvised by the way!

ARNOLD SCHWARZENEGGER

Arnold learned to trust his instincts early. His childhood friends claimed Arnold often said he would accomplish three things in life. He would move to America, become a famous actor, and marry a Kennedy. He accomplished all three. Not bad for someone who grew up in a house with no phone, no fridge and no toilet.

Like Leonardo DiCaprio, Arnold was also advised to change his name for American audiences. He did for his first film, and is credited as Arnold Strong. His accent was so thick at the time, his lines had to be dubbed over.

But as big as Arnold got, there was always a bigger guy. While trying to pay for a dinner he had with 7'4, 500 lbs Andre the Giant, the actor "found himself being physically lifted, and carried back to his table". Andre said simply, "I pay." Hard to argue with someone that huge even if you are Mr. Olympia!

CHRISTIAN BALE

Giving new meaning to the term yo-yo diet! To the concerns of everyone involved in the film, Bale lost an alarming 63 pounds for his role as the emaciated insomniac, Trevor Reznik, in the film, 'The Machinist'. Eating only salads and apples, or simply nothing at all, Bale chewed gum and chain-smoked cigarettes to shed his weight down to an unbelievable 120 pounds!

For his very next film, 'Batman Begins', he then put back on a massive 80 pounds by eating tons of bread, pizza and ice cream. According to Bale, the gorging resulted in more than a few doctor's visits, but he enjoyed the eating so much that he didn't mind getting sick. For these two films, Bale holds the records for the most weight lost for a film role, 63 lbs and for weight gained, 80 lbs.

ROBERT DOWNEY JR.

Speaking of food. During the filming of 'Avengers', Robert

Downey Jr. hid food all over the set so he could eat it unscripted. Apparently nobody could find his hiding spots, so they just let him continue doing it. So when you see him eating in the movie, he's actually eating and offering real food!

The hungry Iron Man theme continued into the final scene of the movie. Downy thought his last line after falling back to Earth was a little boring, so instead of the scripted line "What's next?" Iron Man says to Captain America, "Have you ever tried shawarma? There's a shawarma joint about two blocks from here. I don't know what it is, but I want to try it." So off they went, in full-costume to enjoy a well-deserved meal. You have to watch after the credits to see it. Since then, shawarma sales in Los Angeles, St. Louis, and Boston have reportedly skyrocketed.

ROBIN WILLIAMS

Voted "Least Likely To Succeed"? Hard to believe given the Robin Williams we all know seemed to have an inexhaustible supply of energy, and was of course, very successful indeed. One thing he was well known for was his improvisational skills. In fact, the writers of the Mork and Mindy show purposefully left gaps in scripts for him to work his magic in.

But apparently, sometimes he was too improvisational. The Academy Awards rejected 'Aladdin' for the category of Best Adapted Screenplay because Williams' role in 'Aladdin' was TOO improvised. According to Williams, when he first started recordings, he was just doing the scripted lines, but asked if he could 'try something'. Eighteen hours later, the character of the Genie was finished. As he puts it, I just started playing, and they said "just go with it, go with it, go with it." So he did, and improvised the whole character. In the end, there are about 40 different voices that he did for that role.

WILL SMITH

I guess he's been pranked before. Apparently, when Steven Spielberg called Will Smith to discuss a role in 'Men in Black', Will just wouldn't believe it was actually the legendary director on the other line. But despite Spielberg's involvement in the project, Smith still didn't want the role after he read the script. It was his wife, Jada Pinkett-Smith who finally convinced him to do it.

Smith actually turned down the role of Muhammed Ali as well. However, Ali called Will personally and asked him to take the part, because "he was the only one as good looking as him that could play the role."

Interestingly enough, over a decade earlier, Will Smith (as The Fresh Prince) released the song "I Think I Can Beat Mike Tyson", a fictional and humorous account of his bout with the boxing legend. Then a few years later, recording under his own name this time, he released the song "Gettin' Jiggy Wit It" which contains the line "Met Ali, he told me I'm the greatest." Now that's foreshadowing!

NICOLE KIDMAN

Nicole Kidman was asked to lose as much weight as possible for her role in 'Cold Mountain'. So she went on the 'hard-boiled egg diet'. This is essentially one egg for breakfast, and two to three for dinner. It's not nutritionally advisable in the long run, of course, and Kidman ended up losing more weight than she originally intended.

Hiding from the paparazzi! Apparently, Kidman really loved wearing the prosthetic nose in 'The Hours', so she had fun using it in her private life too. And to hide from the intense public scrutiny during her divorce from Tom Cruise, she used the fake nose and successfully evaded the attraction of hounding photographers.

HEATH LEDGER

A little too real! As the Joker in 'The Dark Knight', Heath Ledger actually frightened people. At the penthouse party scene, where Michael Caine first meets the Joker, he was so startled that he forgot his lines and according to the crew, went white. As Cain puts it, "He frightened the bloody life out of me!" Ledger also had to improvise the line "Look at me!" with Maggie Gyllenhaal because she was so legitimately frightened that she kept trying to look away.

The scary realism came from his commitment to the role. To prepare, he totally immersed himself in the mind of the Joker. He lived alone in a hotel room for six weeks, where he formulated all the fine details of the Joker's psychology. He developed the posture and the voice, and the creepy habit of licking his lips. He also kept a diary, where he captured the Joker's thoughts and feelings. He then used this later to guide his performance on camera.

To avoid any comparison with Jack Nicholson's Joker, he modelled his own version after the psychopaths in 'A Clockwork Orange'. And because he didn't think the Joker would let anyone else put makeup on his face, he applied his own.

RANDOM FUN FACTS

1. From humble beginnings to the stars. As a teenager, Tom Hanks sold popcorn and peanuts at baseball games. Now he has an asteroid bearing his name. The asteroid "12818 TomHanks" was named after him when it was discovered in 1996.

2. Given his role as Willy Wonka, master of all things chocolate and candy, it's a little surprising to hear that Johnny Depp was actually allergic to chocolate as a child.

3. Was Jennifer Lawrence taking method acting lessons from Daniel Day-Lewis? For the film 'Winter's Bone', she actually killed and skinned a squirrel on camera.

4. Outsmarting the press! Daniel Radcliffe deliberately wore the same outfit for 6 months....just to annoy the paparazzi. That way, any photos would just look like the same old shot and couldn't be used. He and Kidman should trade notes!

5. Marlon Brando was famous for refusing to, or not bothering to memorize his lines. In a scene for Superman, where he is speaking to Superman as a baby, his lines were actually written on the diaper!

6. The voice of Darth Vader is so iconic to fans today, but it almost never came to be. Voice actor James Earl Jones had

a severe stutter as a child, and was so ashamed of it that he was silent for nearly 8 years.

7. Many movie fans may know Ewan McGregor for his role as Obi-wan Kenobi in the new Star Wars films. What they might not know is that his uncle fought for the rebellion in the original trilogy. Uncle Denis Lawson portrayed Wedge Antilles in all three original Star Wars films.

8. John Rhys-Davies has had some 'troubles' on his more adventurous shoots. He developed an uncomfortable and itchy skin allergy to his dwarf makeup in 'Lord of the Rings', which caused an extreme reaction on his face. And while filming 'Raiders of the Lost Ark', he caught cholera, which regrettably caused him to crap his own pants while bending over during one scene. Needless to say, that one got deleted.

9. It's well-known that many leading actors resort to camouflage to hide their age. Did you know Sean Connery wore a toupee in all his James Bond movies? He began losing his hair at the age of 17. Privately, and in most of his post-Bond movies, he didn't wear a toupee, but production spent 20,000 dollars on one for 'The Hunt For Red October'.

10. Never a smoker. Although Emma Stone jokes that her husky voice is a result of a smoking habit as a child, it's actually from having colic as a baby. Screaming for 24 hours a day caused calluses to form on her vocal cords, giving her that well-known raspy tone.

11. Now that's a collaboration! For Tom Hardy's role in

'Bronson', Charles Bronson shaved off his actual moustache and sent it to Tom for him to wear.

12. Woody Harrelson's father was apparently a contract killer and served time for allegedly killing a federal judge. According to Woody? His dad was CIA trained.

13. Ethan Hawke is most well-known for his acting and movie roles, but he's also a published author. He's published three books, the most recent one, "Rules For A Knight" having been inspired by fatherhood and the raising of his three children.

14. Before he was ever Jules in 'Pulp Fiction', Samuel L. Jackson was an admitted crack addict. Ironically, he completed a drug rehab program just two-weeks before playing a drug addict in 'Jungle Fever'. Now he has a special clause in his contracts that guarantees him 2 days a week off to play golf. And the producers have to pay! That must qualify for a rags to riches story if ever there was one!

15. Uma Thurman's dad is a professor of Buddhist studies, and named her after the goddess of light and beauty in Indian mythology. It's fitting, don't you think?

16. Before his infamous tiger blood and 'winning' meltdown, Charlie Sheen had to go to extra lengths to appear 'wasted'. For his role as a bloodshot and dishevelled punk in 'Ferris Bueller's Day Off', he stayed up for 48 hours straight to get the right look.

17. Sylvester Stallone's first role was actually in a soft-core porno film called, 'The Party at Kitty and Stud's'. He was paid $200 to play a sex-craved gigolo and appear nude. They renamed it 'The Italian Stallion' after 'Rocky' came out and Stallone became famous.

18. Brad Pitt's career has some strange and ironic coincidences. He tore his Achilles tendon during the production of 'Troy'. The character he played? Achilles. He's also appeared in three movies with the number seven in the title: 'Se7en', 'Seven Years in Tibet' and 'Sinbad: Legend of the Seven Seas'. He's also appeared in three movies with the number twelve in the title: 'Twelve Monkeys', 'Ocean's Twelve' and '12 Years a Slave'. Is his agent a numerologist or something?

19. During filming of 'Rain Man', Dustin Hoffman's self-confidence was more than a little unsettled. Both he and Tom Cruise doubted the movie's potential and jokingly called it, "Two Schmucks in a Car". After three weeks of filming Hoffman wanted out, telling director Barry Levinson, "Get Richard Dreyfuss, get somebody else, because this is the worst work of my life." Hoffman would go on to win his second Best Actor Academy Award for his work in the film.

20. Mel Gibson was mugged the night before his audition for 'Mad Max'. The producers liked his "rugged" look so much they gave him the lead role!

TEST YOURSELF - QUESTIONS AND ANSWERS

1. Before embarking on his acting career, Tom Cruise spent a year studying to be:

A) Priest

B) Pilot

C) Lawyer

2. Keanu Reeves' Hawaiian name means:

A) Soft Breeze

B) The Coolness

C) Warrior

3. Nicole Kidman is reportedly afraid of:

A) Clowns

B) Crowds

C) Butterflies

4. This actor was both the first and the last guest on the David Letterman Show:

A) Bill Murray

B) Al Pacino

C) Christopher Walken

5. Christina Applegate attended the 1989 MTV Movie Awards with which actor? Believe it or not, she dumped him at the event and left with someone else.

A) Brad Pitt

B) Johnny Depp

C) Keanu Reeves

ANSWERS

1. A
2. B
3. C
4. A
5. A

CHAPTER TWO

LIGHTS...CAMERA...ACTION!

Action and adventure time! Through the power of film, we get to join our favourite superheroes, villains, adventurers and warriors. Sometimes the action is so real we forget we are watching a story! So, from battles to chase scenes, showdowns and shootouts, have fun with this trivia from some of the best action and adventure movies around!

PIRATES OF THE CARIBBEAN

Has he been drinking? At first, Johnny Depp's performance as Captain Jack had executives worried, as they thought he was drunk on set. But Depp was actually under the inspiration of Rolling Stones rocker, Keith Richards, and cartoon skunk, Pepe le Pew! He figured that pirates were the 18th century equivalent of rock stars, so it all made sense to him.

Disney execs also wondered if he was playing Captain Jack as a gay pirate. It's hard to say, but perhaps this was because of the flamboyant mannerisms and the excessive makeup. The makeup crew really layered it on while filming scenes in a cave, and since they thought it gave Captain Jack a very cool look, they continued to put it on thick for the remainder of the shoot. It all paid off, of course, and a billion-dollar franchise was borne. The makeup crew had another inside joke that they did as a prank *with* Depp. If you look closely, you can see a small scab on Jack Sparrow's chin. What you'll notice, is it gets bigger and bigger throughout the movie.

Sticky fingers! The other Jack on set, played by two capuchin monkeys, was also a bit of a trouble-maker. In one scene, he is seen "smiling", after eluding Captain Jack and returning an Aztec coin to Barbossa. Barbossa thanks him, and if you watch the DVD special features, you learn this was all entirely unscripted. The crew kept a close eye on their wallets after that one!

FIGHT CLUB

They didn't pull their punches! In the parking lot scene where Ed Norton is meant to hit Brad Pitt as hard as he can, he actually did hit Brad...right in the ear. Originally, it was scripted to be a fake punch, but director David Fincher pulled Norton aside before the scene, and told him to hit Pitt in the ear. The pain was real for Brad, as were the smiles and laughter from Ed.

They were actually drunk too! For the golfing scene, where they are drinking and hitting golf balls on Paper St., the two actors really are as drunk as their characters. And the sound you hear, is the golf balls hitting the side of the catering truck!

Helena Bonham Carter got in on the realism too. She insisted that her makeup artist apply her makeup left handed, as she didn't feel Marla was a person who would be very skilled, or at all concerned with properly applied makeup.

They did have to dial back the realism a little bit though. The book that the film is based on, calls for an actual workable recipe for home-made explosives, but they opted for a fictional one in the interest of public safety.

When filming was done, Pitt didn't want his parents to see the film, but he couldn't convince them not to watch...until they saw the chemical burn scene that is. Don't try this one at home!

INDIANA JONES

Did you catch that? Star Wars fans will love this cameo in 'Raiders of the Lost Ark'. It's easy to miss, but if you look closely, when Indiana Jones and Sallah descend into the Well of Souls, you can see R2D2 and C3PO pop up, not once, but twice....as hieroglyphics. Look at the pillar, where you can see them etched in the stone together. The second one isn't quite as clear, but it shows Princess Leia uploading the plans to the Death Star into R2, just as she did in the actual Star Wars movie. These were uncredited cameos, of course.

The desert scenes for the film were all shot in Tunisia, and apparently, nearly everyone in the cast and crew got sick...except for director Steven Spielberg. It could have been just blind luck, but it's more likely he avoided illness by only eating the food he'd brought with him...a whole lot of cans of Spaghetti-O's.

300

You've gotta be in shape! Especially if you're playing legendary Greek Spartan warriors. And especially if the script demands that the majority of your screen time is to be bare-chested, as it was for most of the cast of '300'. To prepare for their portrayals as the most well-trained fighting force of their time, the entire cast was put through an 8-week training regime prior to shooting. Gerard Butler, who played King Leonidas, said it was the most difficult thing he ever had to do in his life. And he had already spent 2 months prior working out 4 hours a day! Well, it was Sparta!

Different demands were placed on the other actors. For the scene with the Oracle, the flowing effect was achieved by filming the actress dancing under water, and it took five hours every day to apply the hunchback makeup for the character of Ephialtes. It's hard to feel sorry for a traitor though, isn't it?

DIE HARD

A long history. The film was initially intended to be a sequel to another action film, 'Commando', that was released in 1985. And because the original concept of this movie was directly tied to Frank Sinatra, he had to be offered it first. He was too old for the role though, and the stunts would have been too demanding. So, the role of police officer John McClane eventually went to Bruce Willis.

It's a good thing too, as filming was quite physically demanding. One scene where Bruce Willis' character fell down the elevator shaft wasn't actually a scripted stunt. It was a mistake caught on film. Willis has also sustained permanent hearing loss from the incessant firing of guns on set. I suppose he didn't need to hear what they were saying anyways...the German terrorists are not speaking real German, they are actually speaking gibberish.

And that last scene, with the look of pure fear on Alan Rickman's face as he falls to his death...that's genuine fear. Production dropped Rickman 40 feet one second before they said they were going to, in order to capture a look of real terror.

SAVING PRIVATE RYAN

Building camaraderie. For 'Saving Private Ryan', all the main actors were forced to undergo a brutal boot camp for their roles as soldiers. Everyone but Matt Damon that is. Director Steven Spielberg wanted to create genuine resentment towards Damon and his character, and build a strong sense of camaraderie amongst the rest of the cast. The training was so intense that everyone but Tom Hanks voted for a stoppage. Tom had been trained similarly for the Vietnam scenes in 'Forrest Gump', so he had no illusions as to how tough it was going to be. Apparently, he actually enjoyed it. And his vote carried more weight, of course, so they were all obliged to complete the training.

The efforts for realism paid off, and many veterans of D-Day congratulated director Steven Spielberg for the film's authenticity.

X-MEN

A cold start. Apparently actor Hugh Jackman, who played Wolverine in 'X-Men', would take a cold shower every morning before coming to set. He said the shock would make him want to scream, but he couldn't or it would wake his sleeping wife. So he had to grit his teeth and keep it in, which he said put him in the same mentality as his character is in constantly. He found it suitably inspiring.

And talk about getting into character! As Mystique, Rebecca Romijn's make-up took nine hours to apply. It featured 110 custom-designed prostheses, which covered 60% of her body. She couldn't drink wine, use skin creams, or fly the day before filming, as these could all cause changes in her body chemistry, potentially ruining the prosthetics. She also had to keep her costume a secret. When not required to be on set, she had to sit in an isolated windowless room, or "hell", as she put it.

To celebrate on her last day, she brought a bottle of tequila, which the cast and crew shared during a break. Unfortunately, it reacted with her makeup and she vomited blue-colored puke all over Hugh Jackman. He probably had a *warm* shower after that one!

ROCKY

Holding out at all costs. Sylvester Stallone wrote the script to 'Rocky' after being inspired by a boxing match between Muhammad Ali and Chuck Wepner. Wepner wasn't expected to last beyond 3 rounds, but he just wouldn't go away. And the longer he lasted, the more shocked people became. Ali battered him, breaking his nose, and opening multiple lacerations above both eyes. But no matter how hard he hit him, Wepner continued coming forward. And thus, the character of Rocky was born.

Despite being offered $350,000 for the script, Stallone refused unless he would star as Rocky in the film. This was an amazing amount of stubbornness considering he only had $106 dollars in the bank at the time, and was forced to sell his dog because he couldn't afford to feed it.

Of course, we all know Stallone's gamble paid off, but at the time it meant they didn't have a lot of funding for the shoot. Most of the jogging scenes through Philadelphia were shot guerrilla-style. There was no money for permits, nor to buy equipment or pay extras. So when Rocky is running through the food market, the shop keepers are staring...not because they were directed to do so, but because they just didn't know what was going on. They thought it strange that someone would be running through while someone else was filming! And the famous shot, where the shopkeeper throws Rocky an orange... totally unscripted. The owner didn't even know a movie was being filmed, let alone that he would be in it.

Unfortunately for Stallone, he had to be wheelbarrowed to a hospital after pulling a tendon in his leg while shooting these running scenes. But fortunately, they did get the classic scene of Rocky jumping and celebrating after running up the 72 steps up the Philadelphia Museum of Art.

CHARLIE AND THE CHOCOLATE FACTORY

If you've got a sweet tooth, you would have loved working on the set of 'Charlie and the Chocolate Factory'. Nestlé provided 1,850 bars of real chocolate, and the lollipops on the trees; the giant pink sugar canes; and the giant humbugs were all real candy. Even Willy Wonka's colorful cane is filled with actual candy...Nerds candy to be exact.

A chocolate shop in the UK, Choccywoccydoodah, made the chocolate trees, and flowers, but fake chocolate was used for the river area. 800,000,000 litres in fact, and another 150,00 litres for the waterfall. Unlike the chocolate river from the original film in 1971, which soured after only a day, Tim Burton wanted this river to be thick like real chocolate. And odour free!

And those squirrels! No CGI there. Director Tim Burton actually had 40 squirrels trained to crack nuts before they pounce on Veruca Salt.

And did Johnny Depp have a special inspiration for Willy Wonka? Turns out his performance was based on how he imagined former U.S. President George W. Bush would act while stoned!

CATCH ME IF YOU CAN

According to the real Frank Abagnale, Jr., who has a cameo as the French policeman who arrests Leonardo DiCaprio, most of the movie is true fact. At least 80% of it. Although, while some FBI agents did occasionally chase Abagnale, he certainly never called any of them on Christmas. As Abagnale himself says, "Why would I do that? I didn't want the FBI to know where I was." Hard to argue with the logic.

The courtroom scene was different in real life too, and there was never a reunion with his father. After he ran out of the court, Abagnale never saw, nor spoke to his father again.

And in case you missed it, when Tom Hank's character arrives at Frank's room, and he's about to escape with the suitcases full of money...well, the money floating underneath the door is an homage to the "floating feather" from another of Hank's films: Forrest Gump.

TERMINATOR 2: JUDGEMENT DAY

Did you know that OJ Simpson was first considered for the role of the Terminator, but was passed on due to his perceived over-friendliness. Lucky break for Arnold Schwarzenegger, who got the iconic role instead.

When you break down his $15 million salary for the film, and his total of 700 words of dialogue, he was paid $21,429 per word. This means "Hasta la vista, baby" cost $85,716. Incidentally, the world-famous phrase "Hasta la vista, baby" was translated to "Sayonara, baby" in the Spanish version of the film, to preserve the humorous nature.

As a story from the set goes, a female passer-by thought the biker bar was real, and actually wandered on in. Right past all the location trucks, the cameras and the lights. She only realized something was off when she saw Arnold standing in the bar dressed only in boxer shorts. Wondering aloud what was going on, Schwarzenegger replied that it was male stripper night.

And if you found the T-1000 strangely familiar, don't be surprised. Robert Patrick, who played the role, mimicked the head movements of the American bald eagle for the updated Terminator.

SUPERMAN

The role of Krypton's own Kal-El seems to have a special charm. Apparently, Roger Moore once witnessed Christopher Reeve walking through Pinewood Studios in full Superman costume, but Reeve was totally oblivious. He simply didn't notice all the female admirers watching him, but Roger did. And of course, when he did the same thing dressed as Clark Kent...no one paid any attention at all.

But to acquire that same eye-catching physique, Henry Cavill, who now plays Superman in the new instalments, refused to take steroids to muscle up for the role. He also vetoed any digital touch-ups or enhancements to his body for his shirtless scenes. Rather than resort to dishonest trickery, he said he wanted to, "push his body to the limits, to develop his physique into one that was worthy of the character."

And from what his co-star on 'The Immortals', Mickey Rourke tells us, he succeeded. Apparently, Cavill would do 2000 pushups before going in front of the camera. That tires me out just reading that.

And to prepare specifically for the shirtless scenes, Cavill cut his calorie intake from 5000 to 1500 for 6 weeks, to dramatically reduce his body fat and fully embody Superman. After that incredible effort, director Zack Snyder gave him a tub of ice cream and a pizza as a reward!

ONG-BAK: THE THAI WARRIOR

The martial arts adventure 'Ong-bak' was a long time in the making. Lead actor Tony Jaa trained extensively for four whole years in preparation for the film. In it, he performed all this own stunts and not one single wire was used, nor was any CGI added in afterwards.

In the hopes of gaining future work or perhaps a collaboration, the makers of the film introduced some messages to their favourite directors. In the tuk-tuk taxi chase scene, there is graffiti writing on a wall which says, "Hi Luc Besson we are waiting for you", and "Hi Spielberg let's do it together" can be read on the wall in the background of another scene. Seems like Besson and Spielberg have likely missed their chance though, as Tony Jaa has quit acting and is now a practicing Buddhist monk.

FORREST GUMP

Did you ever wonder what Forrest was saying at the Vietnam rally in Washington? In that scene, Gump's microphone gets pulled, and all we see is his mouth moving. But according to Tom Hanks, he actually says, "Sometimes when people go to Vietnam, they go home to their mommas without any legs. Sometimes they don't go home at all. That's a bad thing. That's all I have to say about that."

And in an easy to miss feat of prowess, Tom Hanks never actually blinks during the ping-pong scenes. He wanted to stay in character and knew that Forrest would have taken the advice to, "never take your eye off the ball" quite literally. However, there was no actual ball to look at anyways, it was all CGI.

Here's another little tidbit. The voice of Elvis? That was Kurt Russel, reprising his lead role from the 1979 film 'Elvis'.

GUARDIANS OF THE GALAXY

Quite the cast of characters! Rather than use CGI or performance capture, Zoe Saldana wanted to use makeup for a more realistic portrayal of her character Gamora. I wonder if she would have made the same choice if she had Dave Bautista's role.

To play the character of Drax, Bautista endured five hours of makeup daily, in order to apply 18 prosthetic tattoo pieces. Apparently, Bautista stood the entire time, with no complaints. Eventually, the make-up department whittled the process down to 3 hours, with 90 minutes needed to remove it all after filming wrapped each day.

But no amount of makeup was going to hide Chris Pratt's...ahem, love handles. Pratt felt he had to appear "cut and ripped" like other super heroes, in order to do the role of Star Lord justice. So, he went on a strict diet and training regime and dropped 60 pounds.

And Vin Diesel loved his character, Groot, so much that he didn't want it to end. He was seen at promotions and premieres still wearing the stilts he wore for the role, and a shirt proclaiming "I Am Groot."

RANDOM FUN FACTS

1. Together at last. Heat was the first film to ever feature both Robert De Niro and Al Pacino acting together on screen. They had both starred in 'The Godfather: Part II', but never shared any actual screen time. And in order to make their unfamiliarity as genuine as possible, the two agreed that the scene when their characters first meet shouldn't be rehearsed. We see take #11 in the film.

2. In case you don't speak German, when Indiana Jones is fighting with one of the Nazis in 'Indiana Jones and The Last Crusade', the soldier at the periscope shouts, "The Americans! They fight like girls!"

3. On the last day of their Army Ranger training, the actors of 'Black Hawk Down' received an anonymous letter slipped under their door. It thanked them for all their hard work, and asked them to, "tell our story true". It was signed with the names of the actual Rangers who died in the Mogadishu firefight.

4. Liam Neeson expected 'Taken' to bomb at the box office, but he agreed to take on the role so he could spend four months in Paris. Ironically, not only was the film a massive hit, but it gave Liam a new onscreen image as an action hero.

5. Neither Michelle Rodriguez nor Jordana Brewster had drivers' licenses or even learners' permits before production of 'The Fast And The Furious' began.

6. Apparently, there is someone out there with the job description: "Stunt Burper". Dakota Fanning needed assistance during the filming of 'Man on Fire' because she just couldn't bring one up herself.

7. After seeing the first cut of 'Rambo: First Blood', which was over three hours long, Sylvester Stallone tried to buy the film back so he could destroy it. He was worried it would kill his career. When that attempt failed, he suggested to the producers that they cut out much of his part and let the rest of the characters tell the story. They removed half of the film to what we see today.

8. If you start watching '3:10 to Yuma' at exactly 1:20 PM, the train will arrive at 3:10 PM real time.

9. A producer realized that 'Speed' would be a movie hit when he noticed that audience members would walk backwards to use the bathroom during test screenings. They didn't want to miss any of the action!

10. Getting into it! Brad Pitt and Helena Bonham Carter spent three days recording orgasmic sounds for their unseen sex scenes in 'Fight Club'.

11. Mel Gibson enlisted reserves from the Irish Army for the battle scenes in 'Brave Heart'. But several of the scenes had

to be re-shot as many of the extras could be seen wearing sunglasses and wristwatches.

12. Afraid of snakes? Over 150 rattlesnakes, both real and fake, were used for the snake scene in 'Natural Born Killers'. They filmed it at night so the snakes would be more sluggish in the colder temperatures. Apparently this worked, as most of the snakes actually slept through the scene.

13. According to Tom Hardy, Leonardo DiCaprio made a bet with him that Hardy would get nominated for an Oscar for his role in 'The Revenant'. Hardy didn't think so, so they wagered that the loser of the bet would get a tattoo of the winner's choice. Suffice to say, Hardy now sports a tattoo that reads, "Leo knows everything", in Leo's own handwriting style.

14. Suffering from dysentery, and not up for an extended fight with a sword-wielding maniac, Harrison Ford quietly asked if the scene for 'Raiders of the Lost Ark' could be shortened. Director Steven Spielberg said the only way would be if Indy shot the guy. And so that's just what he did.

15. Did you know that Jennifer Lawrence went temporarily deaf in one ear while shooting 'The Hunger Games'? Apparently this was due to repeated ear infections that resulted from a diving scene and water jets that punctured her eardrum.

16. The V For Vendetta's domino scene, where black and red dominoes form a giant letter V, used 22,000 dominoes. The scene itself lasted only 30 seconds, but it took four

professional domino assemblers 200 hours to set it up.

17. For 'Enemy at the Gates', stars Jude Law and Ed Harris were cast because of the expressiveness of their eyes. As military snipers, their characters were frequently called upon to convey emotion without saying a word.

18. In the scene where Joker blows up a hospital in 'The Dark Knight', he was supposed to walk down the street while the explosion at the hospital began, get on the school bus during the scripted pause, and drive away while the explosion finished. Instead, Heath Ledger improvised and fidgeted with the remote detonator instead, giving the scene that special Joker touch.

19. 'The Departed' is the movie with the most uses of the F-bomb and its derivatives to win the Academy award for Best Picture. How many? 237.

20. Someone was busy! More than 10,000 costumes were made for the cast and extras of 'Gladiator'.

TEST YOURSELF - QUESTIONS AND ANSWERS

1. Arnold Schwarzenegger's first film was:

A) Conan the Barbarian

B) Hercules In New York

C) The Running Man

2. Bruce Willis is known to:

A) Wear his watch upside down

B) Keep a picture of his Grandmother in his pocket

C) Floss between takes

3. The highest grossing film of Brad Pitt's career is:

A) Fight Club

B) World War Z

C) Mr and Mrs Smith

4. Nicolas Cage has a famous uncle named:

A) Francis Ford Coppola

B) Martin Scorsese

C) Steven Spielberg

5. This film is often cited as the least historically accurate of all time:

A) Gladiator

B) Braveheart

C) Kingdom of Heaven

ANSWERS

1. B
2. A
3. B
4. A
5. B

CHAPTER THREE

SCIENCE FICTION & FANTASY

Imagination come to life. Film lets us travel to unseen stars and explore alternate universes. And advancements in technology can now bring us to these 'other worlds' like never before! Check out these fun and interesting facts from the science fiction and fantasy department!

THE LORD OF THE RINGS

It took over 3 years of filming to complete the famous trilogy, so there's bound to be an avalanche of trivia. And there is! There's also a lot of hobbit feet. 60,000 for the first movie alone! And fake ears too...more than 1,600 pairs. These were all "cooked" in a special oven that was in use 24 hours a day, 7 days a week. And the feet were one-time use only, as there was no way to remove them without damage. To keep a black market in hobbit feet from springing up, they were all shredded after use. Although apparently Billy Boyd, who played Pippin, still has a pair.

Some of the actors have truly come to embody their roles, but the Aragorn we know almost never was. Viggo Mortensen replaced another actor at the very last minute, and he wasn't even interested to take the role. It was his son, who was a huge fan of the books, that begged him to do it. Good boy! During production, Viggo estimates he must have "killed" every stuntman at least fifty times.

One actor was ready-made for the films. Actor Christopher Lee was a super fan, and was known to have read the complete trilogy once a year from the time it was published until his death in 2015. He actually met the author J.R.R. Tolkien and had received his blessing to play Gandalf. Lee eventually played the role of Saruman, while Gandalf was performed by Ian McKellen, whom Lee said was better fitted for the part.

You might remember how Gandalf banged his head on a ceiling beam when he first meets Bilbo in Hobbiton. It wasn't scripted that way, but director Peter Jackson loved how McKellen brushed it off and kept going with the scene, so he kept it in the final print.

Speaking of Hobbiton, the village was actually made a year before filming began. Jackson wanted it to look as natural as possible, like it was a real lived-in place. So the garden patches are all real and the grass was maintained by having sheep eat it.

There were details in the color of things too. For instance, the Elves had different colored eyes depending on their race. The Lothlorien Elves had light blue eyes, and the Rivendell Elves were dark blue. And since Orcs have black blood, the actors swilled liquorice-based mouthwash to make sure the inside of their mouths were black as well. At least they would have smelled nice!

HARRY POTTER

The props department for the Harry Potter movies had their work cut out for them too. Daniel Radcliffe, who plays Harry, went through over 160 pairs of glasses for the series, and over 500 wands were created just for 'The Deathly Hallows'. Like the hobbit feet in 'Lord of The Rings', these were carefully monitored, and had to be checked in and out like library books.

Homework on set? Director Alfonso Cuaron wanted to get to know his lead actors before filming, so he had each of them write an essay on their characters from the first person point of view. True to form, Emma Watson (Hermione) turned in a 16-page essay, Radcliffe (Harry) wrote a simple one-page paper, and Rupert Grint (Ron Weasley) didn't write a thing. His excuse? He said that's what Ron would have done.

STAR WARS

Where's the faith George? George Lucas who wrote and directed 'Star Wars: A New Hope' wasn't convinced in the success of his pet project. He thought it would be a flop, so rather than attend the premiere, he went to Hawaii with Steven Spielberg. It wasn't a bad move in the end though, as the two of them came up with the idea for Indiana Jones while on the vacation.

And Lucas wasn't the only one convinced the film would be a failure. Apparently, Alec Guinness hated the movie. He thought the dialogue was rubbish, and came up with the idea to have Obi-wan Kenobi killed. According to Harrison Ford, he and Mark Hamill would often fool around on set, but never when Alex Guinness was around. I suppose you might be grumpy too if you had sand people for neighbours.

Look closely. You might have to slow the speed down, but in 'Empire Strikes Back', you can see that the Millennium Falcon isn't just dodging asteroids. The set designers included a potato and a shoe as a bit of a prank on Lucas.

AVATAR

A lucky break. According to Sam Worthington, he knew nothing about the film when he went in for casting. He wasn't given the name of the director, nor told anything about the script. Thinking it was going to be just another waste of time, he almost didn't show up. He's sure glad he did though. Later, he claims it was easier to learn the Na'vi language than master an American accent. His parents are British, and moved with Worthington to Australia when he was 6 months old.

To get the cast prepared, director James Cameron had the crew spend time in Hawaii, trekking in the jungles and living like a tribe. They had to build their own fires, and spear their own fish to eat. Only during the day though, nights were spent at a Four Seasons hotel. This was all meant to give them a better sense of what it would be like to live in, and move around, a real jungle. The film was done on blue screen, far from any real plant life and without any jungle-themed sets to guide them.

WIZARD OF OZ

Did you know in the critically acclaimed movie 'The Wizard of Oz' that the original casting selection for the role of the Tin Man had to vacate his role? He abandoned the project due to a severe allergic reaction that occurred from the aluminum powder makeup.

Judy Garland's wardrobe has a bit of trivia behind it too. Her famous white dress was actually pink, but appeared white because it was easier to film in Technicolor. And her famous song "Somewhere Over the Rainbow" came in at the Number 1 spot on the American Film Institute's 2004 list of the 100 Greatest Songs in American Films.

Don't scare the kids! Margaret Hamilton's role as the Wicked Witch of the West was so terrifying, the director actually cut most of her scenes and edited them severely.

STAR TREK

The new generation. For the filming of the modern era Star Trek films, British actor Simon Pegg didn't have to audition for the role of Scotty. He simply received an email from J.J. Abrams asking if he would like to do it. Pegg said he would have done the role for free, or would even have paid Abrams to be in the movie, he wanted the role that bad.

Another perfect casting choice was Zachary Quinto as Spock. To prepare, Quinto grew out his hair into a bowl cut and shaved his eyebrows to mimic the original look. He also had his fingers glued together to perfect the Vulcan salute.

Before he fully committed to the role of Captain Kirk, actor Chris Pine sent a letter to William Shatner. In it, he explained who he was and expressed his respect for the elder actor. He got a letter of approval back from Shatner with his blessing to carry on with the role.

John Cho is just right for Sulu. He wasn't sure about taking the part, but got strong encouragement from original Sulu, George Takaei. However, George isn't too happy that Sulu is now a gay character on the show. But only because it wasn't how creator Gene Roddenberry had envisioned him.

2001: A SPACE ODYSSEY

A meeting of minds. Director Stanley Kubrick and author Arthur C. Clarke worked closely together to create this sci-fi classic. Clarke first became aware of the project through a telegram he received from MGM studios. It read:

"STANLEY KUBRICK DR STRANGELOVE PATHS OF GLORY ETC INTERESTED IN DOING FILM ON ETS STOP ARE YOU INTERESTED QUERY THOUGHT YOU WERE RECLUSE STOP"

Clarke replied with the following cable:

"FRIGHTFULLY INTERESTED IN WORKING WITH ENFANT TERRIBLE STOP CONTACT MY AGENT STOP WHAT MAKES KUBRICK THINK I'M A RECLUSE QUERY".

'2001' is also the last movie made about men on the moon before the actual Apollo moon landing missions. This has led to the theory that NASA hired Kubrick to fake the moon landing footage. Whatever the case may be, Kubrick did indeed go out of his way for details, importing several tons of sand that he had washed and painted for the moon surface scenes. Further evidence of this legendary attention to detail are the visible replacement instructions he had written for the explosive bolts in the escape pods.

FIFTH ELEMENT

The character of Leeloo had her own way of talking. In the film, it's called the "Divine Language" and it was an invention by director Luc Besson and Milla Jovovich. It had only 400 words, and Luc and Milla engaged in conversations and wrote letters back and forth to practice it. By the time filming wrapped up, they were able to have complete conversations.

When Bruce Willis' character Korben meets Leeloo for the first time and she begins talking to him in her language, Bruce had no idea she was going to do that, so the reaction we see is real. So was his response, which was totally ad-libbed..."Whoa, lady, I only speak two languages, English and bad English."

And in case you were wondering, Leeloo's full name is "Leeloominaï Lekatariba Lamina-Tchaï Ekbat De Sebat". Thank god they shortened it.

CREATURES COME TO LIFE

You might not recognize actor Andy Serkis to see him, but you're probably familiar with his work. He's the force behind characters like King Kong, Caesar from 'Planet of the Apes', and Gollum from 'Lord of the Rings'. The technology used for these characters is called motion capture, and Serkis performs in a unitard.

For Gollum, Serkis based the desperation and cravings for the ring on the withdrawal pains experienced by heroin addicts. For Gollum's voice, he had to drink bottles upon bottles of what he called, "Gollum juice." This was a mixture of honey, lemon and ginger that he kept on hand to keep his throat lubricated. Apparently, the voice is based on the sound of his cat coughing up a hairball. Yeah, that sounds about right.

At least he didn't actually have to eat whole raw fish, as Gollum does in the film. For that scene, Serkis is actually chewing on a fish shaped lollipop.

ROBOTS COME TO LIFE

The advent of artificial intelligence is a common theme in the world of sci-fi. The most recent example being 'Ex Machina', which is based on Plato's "Allegory of the Cave". Essentially, this means waking up to reality as it actually is.

In the film, the three main characters all have biblical names to match their roles. Ava is a form of Eve, being the first woman; Nathan was a biblical prophet; and Caleb was a spy sent by

Moses to gather information on the Promised Land. This all makes perfect sense when you watch the film.

And if you're wondering about the filming location, yes you can stay the night there. The amazing mansion in the film is actually the Juvet Landscape Hotel in Norway. Just don't forget your key card!

HUNGER GAMES

Apparently, Jennifer Lawrence learned well from her older brothers growing up. According to Liam Hemsworth, Lawrence would purposely eat foods with garlic or tuna fish before any kissing scenes between the two. I suppose that's one way to relieve the pressure from the 100 degree heat they had to film in.

But it's unanimous. The cast has agreed multiple times that the hardest scene to shoot was definitely the sewer scene. Aside from the physical challenges involved, filming lasted three weeks, and because they were filming in actual sewers, the temperatures on set got even hotter than they already were.

Elizabeth Banks was trapped by her own makeup! Because of the lengthy and bejewelled nails that her character had, she couldn't unbutton herself or use the bathroom without assistance.

Fans love to come up with the shipping names for their favourite couples. Brangelina, for Brad Pitt and Angelina Jolie, Kimye for Kanye West and Kim Kardashian, and they've also given us one rather unfortunate one for Katniss and her love interest Peeta...Peenis.

PLANET OF THE APES

In the original film, all the actors playing apes were required to wear their masks, even during breaks and in between shots. It simply took too long to prepare the makeup. So they had to drink liquefied meals through straws. Kim Hunter, who played Zira, found the facial prosthetics made her unbearably claustrophobic. She resorted to taking Valium each morning to get through the makeup sessions.

Mark Wahlberg, who starred in the Tim Burton redux, was so anxious to work with the famous director that he agreed to play any role after only a five-minute meeting. Although, he did refuse to wear a loincloth, as he wanted to leave his days of underwear modelling behind him. Not sure why, but Tim Burton has said that he would rather jump out of a window than direct a sequel to this film.

PAN'S LABYRINTH

This amazing film was almost never made! Director Guillermo del Toro is well-known for compiling books full of notes and drawings about his ideas, which he then uses to create his films. He regards this as "essential to the process." But his entire collection for 'Pan's Labyrinth', years worth of material, was errantly left behind in a cab. To Guillermo, this was the end of the project, but the cab driver realized their importance and was able to track the director down, despite considerable difficulty. Del Toro was convinced that this was a blessing, and forged ahead more determined than ever to make the film.

Apparently, Stephen King attended a screening of the film and sat next to the director. According to Del Toro, King squirmed uncomfortably during the scene when the Pale Man chases Ofelia. As he puts it, "that was better than any Academy Award!"

THE PRINCESS BRIDE

Fame can be hard to live with. Like Mark Hamill who apparently gets called "Luke" wherever he goes, Mandy Patinkin says he hears his most famous line repeated back to him every day of his life.

"Hello. My name is Inigo Montoya. You killed my father. Prepare to die." But thankfully for him, Patinkin actually loves hearing it and isn't bothered by it at all.

The role of the giant Fezzik was originally offered to Arnold Schwarzenegger in the 1970's, who was an unknown actor at the time. But by the time the film was actually made, Arnold was too expensive, so the role went to Andre the Giant instead.

Andre was once asked what his favourite thing about making the film was, to which he replied without hesitation, "Nobody looks at me." It's not often a 7'4, 500lb man can go unnoticed, but he says he felt the cast and crew treated him as an equal, and didn't stare at him because of his massive size. Almost forgot, anybody want a peanut?

E.T.

A team effort. Most of the full-body puppetry for the character of E.T. was performed by a 2'10 stuntman, but a very unique actor was used for the role as well. For the scenes in the kitchen, E.T. was played by a 12-year old boy who was born without legs, but was an expert at walking on his hands.

Foreshadowing. During the Halloween scene where E.T. sees a trick-or-treater in a Yoda costume, he acts as if he recognizes him. Flash forward to 'Star Wars: The Phantom Menace', where you can see E.T. species amongst the senate pods. Look for the scene where the senators are all on their feet shouting.

If you didn't know, E.T.'s face was modelled after poet Carl Sandburg, Albert Einstein and a pug dog. His voice was provided by Pat Welsh, an elderly woman who smoked two packs of cigarettes a day for many years, which gave her voice the quality they were looking for. She was paid $380 for 9 hours of recording work. To fill out the range of E.T.'s "voice", the sound effects crews also recorded 16 other people and various animals, including the sound of director Spielberg's sleeping wife, who had a cold, a burp from a USC film professor, as well as raccoons, sea otters and horses.

RANDOM FUN FACTS

1. The release of the movie 'Gattaca' featured a marketing campaign with promotions offering parents the chance to have their children genetically engineered. Apparently, thousands of people thought it was real and called in to have their offspring signed up.

2. J.K. Rowling hand-picked Alan Rickman to play Snape in the Harry Potter movies. She also gave him special instruction regarding his character. Details that no one else knew about, and information about his true role that wasn't revealed until the final novel.

3. Near death escape1 While filming 'The Edge of Tomorrow' with Tom Cruise, Emily Blunt almost killed them both! During one scene, she missed her mark while driving a minivan, and drove head-on into a tree. Apparently, they both started laughing right after the incident.

4. The Wookie suit worn by Chewbacca in 'Star Wars' is made from actual human hair.

5. None of the actors knew beforehand that the Alien was going to jump out of John Hurt's stomach in 'Alien'. The surprise shows on their faces!

6. Messing with the audience. In 'I Am Legend', when Robert

Neville sees that Fred the mannequin has moved into the street, he calls out to it in shocked disbelief. If you watch closely, you can see its head move a little. During that scene, a mime replaced the mannequin to try and play with people's minds as they watched the film.

7. That crazy staircase you saw in 'Inception'. That's actually a reference to a famous painting by M.C. Escher called the, "Penrose Steps".

8. To research his role as Edgar in "Men in Black", Vincent D'Onofrio watched a lot of bug documentaries. And in order to achieve his character's distinctive walk, he wore braces that prevented his knees from bending, and taped up his ankles.

9. Steven Spielberg nearly made a sequel to 'ET' called 'Nocturnal Fears'. It was going to be revealed that E.T. was actually named "Zreck" and that his people were at war with another alien race who captured and tortured Elliot.

10. The makeup team for 'The Never Ending Story' tried to paint actor Noah Hathaway green, just as Atreyu is described in the book. But, it just wasn't believable. According to Hathaway, "I looked like fungi!"

11. Sean Astin lets us in on a little secret in the extended DVD commentary for 'Lord of the Rings'. When Bilbo drops the one ring before leaving Hobbiton, a magnetized floor prevented the ring from bouncing. The idea was to demonstrate the importance and heavy, heavy weight of the

ring.

12. Product placement pays! The sunglasses used by the Men in Black are the Ray-Ban "Predator 2" glasses. After the film was released, Ray-Ban reported that sales of these glasses had tripled, from $1.6 million dollars to $5 million dollars.

13. Penelope Cruz has played the same character twice. Once in 'Vanilla Sky', and again in the Spanish version of the same film, 'Abre Los Ojos', which means "open your eyes" in English.

14. Ironically, John Rhys-Davies, who plays Gimli the dwarf, is the tallest of the actors in the "Fellowship of the Ring". He is 6' 1.

15. More from the soundstage! That sound you hear of the alien spaceship's weapon exploding at the end of 'Independence Day' was actually created using a recording of singer James Brown screaming.

16. Denzel Washington was offered the role of Spooner in 'I, Robot'. Will Smith got the role, but had Denzel accepted, it would've been the second time he played a previously-married police officer with a bionic left arm who chases down a killer robot! The first time was Parker Barnes in 'Virtuosity'.

17. In the 'Chronicles of Narnia: The Lion, the Witch, and the Wardrobe', Edmund asks if the White Witch can make him taller. He got his wish! In fact, Skandar Keynes grew six and

a half inches during filming.

18. Back breaking realism. Two hundred workers spent two months hand-clearing three square miles of Mexican desert for the movie 'Dune'.

19. Recognize that sound? The motorcycle that Captain Kirk rides in 'Star Trek' makes the exact same sound as the flying cars from the animated series 'The Jetsons'.

20. Remember the scene where Will Smith drags the unconscious alien across the desert and shouts, "And what the hell is that smell?" This was an unscripted line and Smith was actually smelling millions of decaying shrimp from the nearby Great Salk Lake. Apparently, nobody had warned Will.

TEST YOURSELF - QUESTIONS AND ANSWERS

1. In early drafts of the script for 'Empire Strikes Back', Yoda was called:

A) Buffy

B) Master Dosho

C) Zoran

2. In the dystopian thriller 'Children of Men', Michael Caine based his character off of which music legend:

A) Jim Morrison

B) John Lennon

C) Ozzy Osbourne

3. To complete his non-human appearance in 'AI: Artificial Intelligence', Haley Joel Osment had to daily:

A) Use contact lenses that made his eyes appear larger

B) Wear a brace to limit his movement

C) Shave all exposed skin

4. Boba Fett fell into the stomach of this monster in 'Star Wars: Return of the Jedi':

A) The Rankor

B) Bib Fortuna

C) The Sarlacc

5. When Hellboy's makeup is complete, the only part of Ron Perlman's body that you can actually see are his:

A) Fingernails

B) Eyelids

C) Lips

ANSWERS

1. A
2. B
3. C
4. C
5. B

CHAPTER FOUR

THE DIRECTOR'S CUT

The director's role is hugely important for any film. They are responsible for guiding the entire cast and production, and for bringing the vision of the script to life. They select the actors for the various roles and choose locations for our favourite scenes. Sometimes they might seem like mad geniuses, because quite often they are! Check out some interesting trivia from the guys 'behind' the cameras!

THE LEGEND

All thanks to De Niro. As the story goes, famed director Martin Scorsese very nearly gave up his profession after a near overdose in 1978. Scorsese was struggling with a cocaine addiction, but a visit in the hospital from his friend Robert De Niro helped him to turn things around. De Niro convinced him to clean up his life, and come make 'Raging Bull' with him. That film paved the way for both of their successful careers. Scorsese says it was De Niro's persistence to get him back to work that saved his life.

Later in his career, Scorsese heard about Nicholas Pileggi's book "Wiseguy" and phoned up the writer unannounced. "I've been waiting for this book my entire life" he said. To which Pileggi replied, "I've been waiting for this phone call my entire life." And so 'Goodfellas' began.

The now-legendary Steadicam trip through the nightclub kitchen was a happy accident. Scorsese had been denied permission to go through the front entrance, and so he had to improvise an alternative. It's since been copied countless times in other films.

According to Ray Liotta, Scorsese was involved down to the finest detail on set, including the cast's wardrobe. He tied Liotta's tie himself to make sure it was accurate for the film's setting, and made sure every one of Robert De Niro's outfits had a watch and a pinkie ring to go with it. He also made sure that associates of the actual characters were always on set to provide helpful and essential information about the life, people, settings, and moods. Now that's how you create a masterpiece!

THE VISIONARIES

A bold move. The sisters (then brothers) approached Warner Studios with the idea of 'The Matrix', but executives were turned off by the $80 million budget they proposed. The studio agreed to give them $10 million, which they promptly used to film the first ten minutes of the movie. This is the opening scene with Carrie-Anne Moss, who plays Trinity. After seeing the scene, the studio green lit the original budget. Coincidentally, that opening action sequence took six months of training and four days to shoot.

Many viewers complained that scenes in the Matrix had a green hue to them. It's true, but this was done on purpose. You'll notice that the scenes that take place within the Matrix have a green tint to replicate the effect of watching them through a computer monitor. Scenes taking place in the "real world" have a blue tint. The fight scene between Morpheus and Neo is tinted yellow, as it is neither in the real world nor in the Matrix.

And if you look closely at the Oracle's apartment, you'll see a sign above the door that reads, "Temet Nosce" which is the Latin for "know thyself". Quite fitting for an oracle. She also gives Neo a literal and metaphorical cookie. Computer nerds know that 'cookies' are small files stored on a user's computer.

AN AMERICAN ICON

There's always a solution. Steven Spielberg was the first person to suggest a PG-13 rating for films. He wanted to address complaints made by parents over the PG ratings of his movies like 'Poltergeist', and 'Indiana Jones and the Temple of Doom'. The move didn't hurt the box office either!

Spielberg rarely does auditions. Instead, he casts actors based on their performances in other works. When a phone call didn't work, he flew Will Smith to his Hampton's home via helicopter to offer him the part in 'Men in Black'. And when he saw Vince Vaughn in 'Swingers', he knew he wanted him for 'Jurassic Park'.

When asked which films he would like to be remembered for, he said 'E.T. the Extra-Terrestrial' and 'Schindler's List'. He actually submitted 'Schindler's List' to fulfill his college graduation requirements and finally get his degree. He was only 33 years late!

Sometimes you have to get creative. To have Amy Adams kiss Leonardo DiCaprio in the sloppy way he wanted for a scene in 'Catch Me If You Can', he told her to pretend she was starving to death and eating a cheeseburger. That's one way to inspire your actors!

THE PERFECTIONIST

A different kind of boot camp. 'Dark Knight' director Christopher Nolan had cast and crew undergo a "movie boot camp", so they could understand the tone he was trying to achieve. For the first four days of production they watched, in chronological order: 'King Kong', 'Citizen Kane', 'Cat People', 'Stalag 17', 'Black Sunday', 'A Clockwork Orange', 'Heat' and 'Batman Begins'.

Like many other successful directors, Nolan seems to have an obsession with detail. For 'Memento', he wasn't satisfied with the way Joe Pantoliano delivered Teddy's line, "You don't have a clue, you freak!" So he re-recorded the last two words to his liking. In the final cut of the film, the words, "you freak," are actually being said by Nolan impersonating Pantoliano's voice.

But details pay off! For a cornfield scene in 'Intersteller', Nolan grew 500 acres of corn, which he learned was feasible from his work as producer on 'Man of Steel'. He sold the corn afterwards and actually made a profit.

DEVOTED CRAFTSMEN

Some directors really go out of their way to make things sound as realistic as they can. Here's some fun examples:

The roar of the T-Rex dinosaur in 'Jurassic Park' was made by layering the sounds of a tiger, an alligator, and a baby elephant over each other.

For the sound of the T-1000 passing through metal bars in 'Terminator 2', they inverted an open can of dog food and recorded as it slowly oozed out. And when the T-1000 was transforming and flowing like mercury, the "metallic" sound is actually Dust-Off being sprayed into a mixture of flour and water, with a condom-sealed microphone submerged in the goo.

The sounds for Harry's unfortunate bathroom scene in 'Dumb and Dumber' were actually recorded at a truck stop. The sound techs for 'Harold and Kumar' got recordings in the same way for the women's washroom scene in 'Harold and Kumar Go To White Castle'.

After 'Dumb and Dumber' premiered, Clint Eastwood approached Jeff Daniels at a celebrity golf tournament, and told the actor that the embarrassing toilet scene actually happened to him in real life. Apparently Clint ate some bad shellfish while on a date and fled to the bathroom only to find out it was broken...after he had used it!

THE MAESTRO

Some of us call it "crazy for detail", but Ridley Scott refers to it as "layering". And who are we to argue? For the set of 'Blade Runner', the level of detail was taken to a new level. Scott had

"Driver is Armed; Carries No Cash" written on the door of a random bus, and had parking meters read in tiny print:

"WARNING - DANGER! You Can Be Killed By Internal Electrical System If This Meter Is Tampered With". Scott also made sure to put the rate on the meters, which was $3 for 1 minute of parking. I guess prices go way up in the future!

The magazine racks even carried creative 21st Century titles like, Krotch, Zord, Bash, Creative Emotion and Droid. And there was even an adult magazine called Horn that had headlines reading "The Cosmic Orgasm", "Hot Lust in Space", "Tit Job Review" and "Scratch and Sniff Centre-Spread".

If you look closely, just outside of the eye scientist's lab, on the left hand side of the door, you can see some graffiti in Asian characters. It reads: "Chinese good, Americans bad." The setting of the movie is one where the population of America is predominately Asian, so this makes sense.

Apparently Ridley Scott was unhappy with the lighting during the first two weeks of filming, so he ordered everything to be done again...from scratch. The decision created conflicts to be sure, but it also created an amazing cinematic experience for the viewers.

THE REBEL

Quentin Tarantino is considered a bit eccentric, so there are many interesting facts to be shared. Here's some of them:

He has a strong distaste for product placement in films, so he likes to come up with fake ones for his own projects. Hence the infamous Kahuna Burger from Pulp Fiction, and others like Red Apple Cigarettes, and Jack Rabbit Slims.

He is regularly seen driving around his home town of Malibu in the famed 'Pussy Wagon' from Kill Bill.

Tarantino worked on the script for 'Inglourious Basterds' for nearly a decade. He almost abandoned the project when he couldn't find anyone to play the role of Colonel Hans Landa. He feared he'd written a role that was unplayable, until he met Christoph Waltz and knew he had his man.

An interviewer once asked why he had misspelled the word bastard in the title of the film, to which he responded, "Here's the thing. I'm never going to explain that. You do an artistic flourish like that, and to explain it would just take the piss out of it and invalidate the whole stroke in the first place."

Quentin wrote the script for 'Natural Born Killers' but disowned the film afterwards, claiming he hated the final version. Until a chance meeting that is. As the story goes, he bumped into Johnny Cash in an elevator and Cash told him that both he and his wife June were big fans, and that they especially liked 'Natural Born Killers'. I guess Tarantino is a big Johnny Cash fan.

Tarantino says he likes to leave 20% of his movies 'unseen'. He wants the viewer to feel like the movie is really theirs. A good example of this is not showing what's in the suitcase in 'Pulp Fiction'. It's true, that one spawned a thousand internet theories!

By the way, the 'Bad Mother F*cker' wallet seen in 'Pulp Fiction' actually belonged to Quentin.

PASSION PROJECT!

Some directors will stop at nothing to get their film to the screen. To make his cult-classic 'Pi', Darren Aronofsky raised the necessary $60,000 from individual $100 contributions. Mostly from friends and family. There was no money to secure location permits, so one of the crew was constantly serving as a lookout for police. This way they could stop filming and avoid detection when necessary. His mom also did the catering for the film to keep costs down.

'Pi' was later bought by Artisan Entertainment, which allowed Aronofsky to give his contributors a $150 return on their investment. Darren also started a tradition with 'Pi'. He doesn't shave his beard until production is complete and filming is wrapped.

His films are known for their vividness and powerful emotional effect. This is often due to the realism he strives for. After watching a screening of 'The Wrestler', former WWF star Roddy "Rowdy" Piper apparently broke down and cried.

CREATING A MASTERPIECE

Director Michael Mann was head honcho at the helm for the heist classic 'Heat', which starred Robert De Niro and Al Pacino. In order to get insight into prison life, and to develop and flesh out the main characters, Mann paid several visits with inmates in

Folsom Prison. He also arranged for the cast to meet with real life LAPD detectives and professional criminals.

Cast playing cops dined with the LAPD and their wives on one night, and cast playing thieves had dinner with criminals and their wives on a separate night. Mann wanted the actors to have a better idea how these different groups interacted and socialized, and it really shows up in the film.

The average viewer probably wouldn't notice, but the main gangster Neil always had perfectly starched collars on his shirts. Mann had learned that this is how it is in prison. And his grey colored suits were also specially selected to help him blend into crowds and not draw attention to himself. These are the kind of details that create the total atmosphere and texture of the film.

For the epic gunfight scene, Mann installed microphones all over the set to capture the audio live. He didn't want to have to dub the gunshots in afterwards. This added to the impact of the scene and it sounds like no other gunfight ever shown on screen before. For that one scene, they used from 800 to 1000 rounds of blank ammunition a take.

THE NEUROTIC GENIUS

Just like Johnny Depp, Woody Allen refuses to watch any of his movies once they are released. Not sure if this is one of his phobias, but we could probably add it to the list. Among his "collection" of neuroses are: arachnophobia (spiders), entomophobia (insects), heliophobia (sunshine), cynophobia (dogs), altophobia (heights), demophobia (crowds), carcinophobia (cancer), thanatophobia (death), and misophobia (germs). He also admits to being terrified of hotel bathrooms.

He must have some interesting allergies as well. The scene in 'Annie Hall', where Woody sneezes into the cocaine was actually an unscripted accident. When previewed, however, the audience laughed so loud that director Allen decided to leave it in. He had to add extra footage to compensate for people missing the next few jokes from laughing so hard.

Not until the success of 'Midnight in Paris', did Woody actually make his fortune from film making. Before then, he had earned more money from selling real estate than he had from all of his movies combined.

FAMILY MAN

Francis Ford Coppola and two of his masterpieces: 'The Godfather' and 'Apocalypse Now'.

'The Godfather' was truly a 'family' affair. Not only is it about "The Family", meaning the organized Italian crime families in New York, but Francis Ford Coppola worked with his own relatives in the film. His sister, Talia Shire, played Connie Corleone, his mother was an extra in the restaurant scene, his father, Carmine, is the piano player in the mattress sequence, and his sons are extras as well. The baby boy who gets baptized? That's actually his daughter Sofia, who would go on to become an established director in her own right.

The film had its challenges. Studio executives were firmly set against Marlon Brando playing the title role. So Coppola had to fight for his choice of cast, and the studio relented, but only upon 3 conditions:

1) That Brando do the movie for free

2) That he perform a screen test

3) If he put up a $1 million bond that he will in no way have any misbehavior that would cause an overrun of the budget.

As the story goes, Coppola said, "I accept," ...meaning he couldn't talk about it at the moment. Well, suffice to say, Brando got the role and went on to win the Academy Award for Best Actor for his portrayal of Vito Corleone.

Coppola and author Mario Puzo worked together on the script to get it just right. For the scene where Clemenza is cooking, Coppola originally wrote, "Clemenza browns some sausage." When Puzo saw this, he crossed out "browns" and replaced it with "fries," writing in the margin, "Gangsters don't brown."

'Apocalypse Now' is as legendary for its many troubles on set as it is for its powerful and psychedelic cinematic experience. There were many delays during filming, and some of the cast were using drugs and alcohol to considerable excess. Somehow Al Pacino had a sense of this before it all began. When Francis Ford Coppola asked him to play the main character of Willard, Pacino turned him down saying, "I know what this is going to be like. You're going to be up there in a helicopter telling me what to do, and I'm gonna be down there in a swamp for five months." He was right, but the shoot actually lasted sixteen months.

In the end, Coppola had to invest several million dollars of his own money to keep the project going, and had to mortgage his home and winery in Napa Valley in order to finish. He lost 100 pounds while filming, and threatened suicide several times during the making of the film.

FROM MONTY PYTHON TO 12 MONKEYS...VIA BRAZIL

For the Japanese release of 'Monty Python and the Holy Grail', "Holy Grail" is translated to "Holy Sake Cup." Director Terry Gilliam cut his chops directing the British comedy troupe, and like Francis Ford Coppola, had to go to war against studio executives to get what he wanted on the screen.

Apparently, Universal Studios refused to release the film 'Brazil' with Gilliam's original ending. They wanted a happy ending, aka the "Love Conquers All" ending. To get his way, Gilliam held secret screenings of the film and invited the top critics to attend. With the support of the critics behind Gilliam, the studio relented and released the film as Gilliam designed it. But it didn't come without a cost. All the stress caused him to lose feeling in his legs for a week!

For '12 Monkeys', Gilliam was concerned that Brad Pitt wouldn't be able to channel the nervous, rapid speech he was looking for. After a speech coach didn't work, he just took away Pitt's cigarettes, and Pitt played the part exactly as Gilliam wanted.

In a rather unique piece of directing, Gilliam gave Bruce Willis a list of "Willis acting cliches" that he was forbidden to use during filming. One of these was the "steely blue eyes look". Perhaps this is where Ben Stiller got the idea of Blue Steel for 'Zoolander'.

A NEW KIND OF PITCH

Director Zack Snyder took a unique approach to get funding for the action film '300'. First he took all the images from Frank Miller's graphic novel that the movie was based on, and scanned them into a computer. After removing the dialogue and descriptive text, they added simple animation effects, like moving clouds, sparkling eyes, and a burning bush. Then they edited them into an animated comic strip. The finishing touch was a voice-over narration.

But even this wasn't enough to open the studio purse strings. So, to convince Warner Bros that they could indeed make the film, they shot a live-action 'test' sequence involving a Spartan warrior killing several Persians in a 360-degree continuous shot. This finally did the trick and Snyder went on to make the visually stunning film of the famous Greek heroes.

THE ECCENTRIC

You might not have guessed it from his body of work, but director Tim Burton had a very typical suburban upbringing in his Burbank, California home. Perhaps it was the boredom though that inspired young Tim to spend his time crafting very twisted and imaginative drawings. Well, they weren't for naught. Some of these drawings became the inspiration for his most memorable characters, like Edward Scissorhands and movies like 'The Nightmare Before Christmas'.

And Burton hasn't given up his art as an adult either. He often displays his work in art galleries and special exhibitions around the world. He and Johnny Depp swapped sketches of the Mad Hatter character prior to filming 'Alice in Wonderland' to get just the right look.

For 'Sleepy Hollow', Burton and the crew built an entire small town to film in, complete with rooms, floors, and stairs. According to the cast and crew, "The feeling one had walking around the 'Sleepy Hollow' sets, and in particular the town at Lime Tree, was almost as if you were walking around the inside of Tim Burton's head."

THE MYTHICAL AND THE MYSTERIOUS

During the filming of 'The Shining', director Stanley Kubrick would reportedly call up author Stephen King at odd and late hours to ask him questions about the book. According to King, Kubrick asked him one time, "Do you believe in God?" When King replied that he did, Kubrick yelled "I knew it!" and slammed the phone down.

His last film, 'Eyes Wide Shut', was shrouded in secrecy. For just one minute of footage actually used in the film, Kubrick had Kidman shoot six days of naked sex scenes with a male model, having the pair pose in over 50 erotic positions. While this was being filmed, he banned her then-husband, Tom Cruise, from the set. He also forbade Kidman from sharing with him what happened during the erotic scene. This was a technique he was using to exaggerate a sense of distrust and jealousy between the couple they were playing. He wanted to capture the erosion of trust on film.

According to Arthur C. Clarke, who worked closely with Kubrick for '2001: A Space Odyssey', Stanley attempted to get a very unique insurance policy from Lloyds of London. He wanted to protect himself from any potential losses in the event that alien life was discovered before the movie was released.

Lloyds refused.

RANDOM FUN FACTS

1. According to Martin Scorsese, Marlon Brando tried to persuade him not to make 'Goodfellas'. Thankfully for us film fans, Martin didn't listen.

2. Peter Weir had a crazy idea. When 'The Truman Show' was preparing for release, Weir wanted to install cameras in every theatre the film was to be shown in. This would allow him to have the film stopped at a certain point to then display the live audience to themselves on the big screen. Thus creating an authentic Truman experience for the moviegoers.

3. Which pill would you take? The Blue one and go back to sleep in the Matrix, or the Red one and wake up to reality as it is? When asked, the Wachowskis revealed that they'd both take the Blue Pill when given Neo's choice.

4. Marion Cotillard was such a big fan of Tim Burton that she slept with the script for 'Big Fish' under her pillow for a month until she got the part.

5. The rock band Led Zeppelin doesn't let just anyone use their music. Director Richard Linklater knew this, so he filmed a special request by actor Jack Black in front of 1000 screaming fans imploring the band to let them use

"Immigrant Song" in 'The School of Rock'. It worked!

6. Building chemistry? In order to get Amy Adams and Joaquin Phoenix to know each other better for the film 'Her', director Spike Jonze essentially locked them in a room to talk for hours on end.

7. 'Mad Max' director used one of his own cars to be destroyed when the budget for the film started to balloon.

8. Quentin Tarantino literally scratched the physical film for 'Death Proof' to achieve the "dirty" aesthetic he was after.

9. Nicole Kidman gave co-star Natalie Portman some advice on the set of 'Cold Mountain'. "Always choose a film by its director. You're never certain how the movie will turn out, but you are always guaranteed an interesting experience". This explains why Kidman took the role for 'Eyes Wide Shut' without even looking at the script. Stanley Kubrick was a director she wanted to work with.

10. During the filming of 'Harry Potter', director Alfonso Cuarón inspired a needed look of awe out of Daniel Radcliffe by telling him, "Pretend you're seeing Cameron Diaz in a G-string". It worked!

11. While filming the deli scene for 'The Wrestler', real customers kept walking up to the counter looking to buy meat and cheese. Director Darren Aronofsky told Mickey Rourke to take their orders and improvise while the camera rolled. This is the footage used in the film.

12. Judd Apatow's first job was as a dishwasher in a comedy club. He took it so he could meet stand-up comics and make movies with them! He did and he does!

13. Francis Ford Coppola urged his daughter Sofia to shoot 'Lost In Translation' in High Definition Video, because "it's the future". She opted for film because, as she puts it, "film feels more romantic".

14. Most of the actors for '12 Monkeys' took a pay cut just so they could get the chance to work with Terry Gilliam. They must have been listening to Nicole Kidman's advice on choosing a film because of its director!

15. 'Almost Famous' is actually director Cameron Crowe's semi-autobiographical account of life as a young Rolling Stone reporter. Crowe first toured with The Allman Brothers Band, who distrusted him, and kept asking if he was a narc. Just like Stillwater in the movie did.

16. Christopher Nolan has never had a movie rated as "rotten" on Rotten Tomatoes, and his lowest rated movie is 'The Prestige' at 76 percent.

17. Quentin Tarantino served in jail three times for parking tickets. He was too poor at the time to pay for them.

18. No improvisation. When an actor improvises a line on a Coen brothers set, they're likely to hear, "That was great, but could you do it like it's written in the script?" The Coen brothers stick to the scripts that they write, which even

include "uhs" and "hmms".

19. Ridley Scott cast Rutger Hauer in 'Blade Runner' without ever meeting the actor. But Rutger punked the famed director by showing up wearing huge green sunglasses, pink satin pants and a white sweater with an image of a fox on the front. Apparently, Ridley turned white!

20. Double role as conductor. To get the powerful effect of 10,000 Uruk-Hai orcs performing their battle chant at Helm's Deep for 'Lord of the Rings', Peter Jackson led a stadium crowd of 25,000 cricket fans through the sequence of "Derbgoo, nashgshoo, derbgoo, dashshoo," spelled out on the jumbo screen.

TEST YOURSELF - QUESTIONS AND ANSWERS

1. Which character did director Kevin Smith play in 'Clerks'?

A) Jay

B) Silent Bob

C) Dante Hicks

2. Wes Craven was the director behind which horror franchise?

A) Hostel

B) Saw

C) A Nightmare On Elm Street

3. This director often plays the piano scores for his films:

A) David Lynch

B) Clint Eastwood

C) David Fincher

4. Which film isn't a Wes Anderson creation?

A) The Royal Tenenbaums

B) The Grand Budapest Hotel

C) The Occidental Therapist

5. Which director can't return to America or he will be arrested?

A) Roman Polanski

B) David Cronenberg

C) Terrence Malik

ANSWERS

1. B
2. C
3. B
4. C
5. A

CHAPTER FIVE

ANYTHING FOR A LAUGH

Comedians make us laugh. It's simple and obvious, but it's the plain truth, and we love them for it. After all, can you imagine a world without laughter? We can't, and we wouldn't want to. So we thought you'd like these interesting facts from some of the greatest comedians around. Enjoy!

THE FRAT PACK

An assembly of jokesters. "The Frat Pack" is the nickname given to the group of comedy actors who have been making hilarious movies together for the past couple decades. Ben Stiller, Jack Black, Owen Wilson, Will Ferrell, Vince Vaughn, and Steve Carell are all honorary members.

Remember Frank the Tank's streaking scene from 'Old School'? Will Ferrell was actually fully naked for this one. He says he knew it was the right move after he heard shrieks of pure horror when he dropped his robe. The scene was filmed in public view across the street from a 24-hour fitness centre! Apparently the presence of Snoop Dogg on set was intimidating, so he resorted to some "liquid courage" to get the job done. And the 'naked clause' from the contract? It gave the film the right to use his naked image "in any part of the universe, in any form, even that which is not devised."

Another movie that had the gang all together was 'Anchor Man: The Legend of Ron Burgundy'. The version we get to see on screen was not actually the original vision for the plot. The first draft of the script was actually a tale of monkeys and cannibalism. The story started with the collision of two planes in the remote mountains. One plane had the Channel 4 News Team aboard, and the other was full of monkeys and martial arts equipment. I suppose the rest would have to be improvised.

THE BIG LEBOWSKI

Was he a prophet? This Coen brothers classic actually spawned a religious movement based on the Dude called, "The Church of the Latter-Day Dude". They must drink Caucasians instead of holy wine.

The film's characters were big into bowling so promoters in Norway played on this fact. Posters for the film included the text "Anbefales av norsk bowling forbund" (Recommended by the Norwegian Bowling Association).

And believe it or not, every single utterance of "man" and "dude" was written right in the script. The Dude actually says "man" 147 times in the movie at an average of nearly 1.5 times per minute. "Dude" is used 161 times, and the F-word or variation of it is used 292 times. Although, this number isn't as high in one version that was edited for television broadcasts. The famous line "This is what happens when you f**k a stranger in the ass!" was changed to "This is what happens when you find a stranger in the Alps!"

THE HANGOVER

From Frat Pack to Wolf Pack. The Hangover series is one of the most commercially successful comedies of all time. And with all the big-name actors in the film, one guy might have gone unnoticed, except of course, he is one of the greatest boxers of all time. Mike Tyson has since revealed that he took the role to fund his drug habit at the time. According to Tyson, he was high on cocaine during the filming of all his scenes. But in the end, it was working on the film that convinced him to make changes in his life.

The first film was set in Las Vegas, and has had an interesting cultural impact on the city. Staff at Caesars Palace report that they are repeatedly asked two famous lines from the film: "Did Caesar live here?" and, "Do you know if the hotel is pager friendly?" They've even had inquiries from guests looking to recreate some of the film's wildest scenes, including ones with a tiger. They might have to speak to Iron Mike for that one...in real life, Mike Tyson owns seven tigers.

A GREEN OGRE AND A DONKEY

The Shrek series is hugely popular, but what if he wasn't Scottish? Mike Myers, the voice of Shrek, originally recorded the role using his natural speaking voice. Something didn't feel right though, so he re-recorded with a Scottish accent inspired by the voice his mother used when she read him bedtime stories as a child.

The re-do cost $4 million dollars, and when Myers realized he had forgotten the line, "What are you doing in my swamp?!" they had to record it from the back of a limo while driving through New York City.

Remember the scene where Princess Fiona lets out a huge burp? They wrote that into the film after Cameron Diaz was burping while drinking Coca-Cola during a recording session. She even broke out into Cantonese during her Kung Fu fight with Robin Hood and his Merry Men.

And the production very nearly lost its art director. While visiting a magnolia plantation to get ideas for Shrek's swamp, he ended up getting chased by an alligator! Thankfully, he made it to safety.

HE FOOLED YOU

Very nice! British comedian Sacha Baron Cohen rose to fame with the cast of characters he used to fool the unwitting public. While filming 'Borat', the police were called ninety-two times, and the FBI even had a team assigned to him due to numerous reports of a "Middle eastern man traveling the Midwest in an ice cream truck".

The character Borat was actually based on a Russian doctor that Cohen had met. He described him as completely, but unintentionally hilarious. Well, that is Borat. It takes Sacha 6 weeks to grow all the required Borat body, head and facial hair. For Ali G, the white gangster from Staines, it takes only 4 weeks to grow the goatee, and when preparing to play Bruno, he actually shaves his entire body.

Unfortunately, Cohen has had to retire his characters as they are now far too famous to fool anyone anymore. Even Bruno, the gay Austrian fashion reporter, who once crashed a fashion show in Milan using fake IDs has been retired. He received a quick escort off the premises by security who quickly recognized the 'trouble maker'.

SHAUN OF THE DEAD

Isn't it obvious? When asked why they opted to use slow moving zombies instead of the normal running zombies, Simon Pegg (Shaun) simply replied, "Because death is not an energy drink."

And remember the scene where Shaun tells his girlfriend that he's going to take her to "the place that does all the fish"? How romantic right? But if you look closely when he opens the phone book, you can see the restaurant is really called, 'The Place That Does All the Fish'.

Nick Frost (Ed) allegedly shaved his genitals for the entire production to create a genuine need for his character to keep scratching. That's a method acting first!

The cause of the zombie apocalypse is never properly explained in the movie. Whenever anyone is about to do so, they keep getting interrupted by something else. But if you listen to the scene where Shaun is headed to the shop for the first time, you can hear a newscast over the radio mentioning a space probe that unexpectedly re-entered Earth's atmosphere and exploded over England. This is also a subtle homage to 'The Night of the Living Dead' which had a similar plot theme.

CLERKS

His movie was his life. Writer, director and star Kevin Smith actually worked in the store where they shot the film, and the cast is a group of all of his friends. He would start work at 6am and finish at 11pm, when they would then shoot the scenes for the movie until 4am. Next day...back to work. He kept this up for the 21 straight days they needed to film the scenes.

And to finance the $27,000 needed for the film, Smith sold a large part of his prized comic collection. He's since gone on to huge commercial success and has been able to buy most of it back. He also borrowed from his parents and maxed out his credit cards. Good thing his gamble paid off!

Smith has said that he cast himself in the movie in case it was a huge flop. That way, if he had to live with the permanent debt for the rest of his life, "he could at least point to his face in the movie as proof that he actually did it."

TEAM AMERICA WORLD POLICE

ARE.....PUPPETS?

Pranking the studio. The film's creators, Trey Parker and Matt Stone, decided to mess around with the executives at Paramount Studios. And it worked! When asked for a sample from the film, the pair showed the studio heads footage of a poorly-crafted puppet in front of a very badly drawn Eiffel Tower. Allegedly one of the executives shouted, "Oh God, they f**ked us!"

Of course, it was just a joke, and they quickly pulled the shot back to reveal a highly-refined marionette manipulating an inferior one, followed by a fly-over of a beautifully designed Parisian landscape full of other well-made marionettes. This ended up being the opening sequence of the movie.

And if you look closely, there are all kinds of fun details in the film. The jungle background in the Panama scenes is all cannabis plants, and in the Paris scene, the streets are actually paved with croissants. The statue in Kim Jong-il's palace is actually just a human in heavy makeup, and if you pay attention, you can see his eyes blinking. The directors also used household objects as props to remind the audience of the actual size of the puppets being used. You'll find a pair of nail clippers on a Team America's utility belt in their first scene, and in Cairo, one puppet is carrying a basket of Goldfish snacks on his head.

Kim Jong-il, the notorious leader of North Korea, and a famous movie buff, has never publicly commented on the film, nor his prominent role in it. We'd like to think he was a fan.

WAYNE'S WORLD

Schwing! For the now famous "Bohemian Rhapsody" sequence, Mike Myers almost used a Guns and Roses song instead. Probably wouldn't have helped their necks any better. Both Myers and co-star Dana Carvey developed severe pain in their necks from all the head-banging involved. You can see the effects of this in later scenes, where they are both trying to move their necks as little as possible.

And that wasn't all for Carvey. He stated in interviews that he developed severe pain in his jaw from Garth's extreme overbite. When filming wrapped each day he had to hold bags of ice on either side of his face! And the dream woman? Sorry Garth, she's been Dan Aykroyd's wife since 1983.

But the pain didn't stop Carvey from improvising. For the scene when Wayne and Garth are watching planes fly overhead, there was a lull while waiting for the next incoming plane. To kill the time, Carvey spontaneously asks Wayne if he ever thought Bugs Bunny was attractive in women's clothing. The laughter was genuine, so they decided to keep the dialogue in the film.

FORGETTING SARAH MARSHALL

Not afraid to share. Some of the scenes from this comedy favourite have real-life inspiration. Screenwriter and star Jason Segel explained that both the naked breakup scene and the Dracula puppet musical show were drawn from his real-life experiences. But he wasn't devastated by the breakup like his character was in the film. Apparently, he thought it was totally hilarious and he couldn't wait for the girl to leave so he could write it all down!

Segel also thought it would be funny if he didn't tell his mom about the naked scene. Apparently, she didn't find it very funny and actually cried in the theatre. Afterwards, she sent a warning email to other family members, but did say that the scene was "essential to the plot".

And before he was a successful actor, Segel was really working on a musical adaptation of "Dracula"... using puppets. Segel had jokingly mentioned to director Judd Apatow that they use this as a plot device, but Apatow liked the idea, so they put it in.

SNATCH

What's he saying? Brad Pitt was a huge fan of 'Lock, Stock and Two Smoking Barrels', so when he heard Guy Ritchie was making another film, he called the director up to see if there was a role in it for him. Ritchie instinctively said yes, but he realized after that he'd offered Pitt a role in 'Snatch' that didn't actually exist. So he rewrote the script with a part just for Brad...Mickey O'Neil. But then he found out Pitt couldn't quite master the London accent, so he had the character speak an indecipherable accent. One that even the other characters couldn't understand. This was his way of responding to criticism he'd received over the accents in his first film.

Pitt got right into the role of Mickey, and because it was a particularly scummy character, he made a specific point of not washing much during production. It worked for his hair, but much to the chagrin of the rest of the cast.

FEAR AND LOATHING IN LAS VEGAS

Spitting image. Actor Johnny Depp had much respect for Hunter S. Thompson, whose adventures and novel the movie is based on. The two quickly became friends and Depp spent four months living with Thompson, studying his mannerisms and learning the proper vocal inflections. Thompson even lent much of the clothing Depp wore in the film; actual hats and shirts he himself had worn in the '70s. He even shaved Depp's head in his kitchen, wearing a miner's hard hat for the job so he could see properly and do a professional job.

The result was a hearty approval from Thompson who once remarked, "If he ever saw anyone acting the way Depp does in the film, he would probably hit them with a chair."

JIM CARREY

What's with his mouth? Those oversized teeth that the Mask character had were originally props just to be used during silent scenes. But Jim thought they would add an extra dimension of wackiness, so he learned to talk with them in.

He went the extra mile in 'Liar, Liar' too. When his character Fletcher beats himself up in the restroom, that was really the sound of Jim's head slamming into the urinal, floor and walls. No sound effects were used!

Apparently they were both inspired by animals! During a dinner together, Jim and actor Anthony Hopkins discovered they each based a character's movements on animals. Ace was based on birds and Hannibal Lecter on reptiles. Carrey confessed that Hopkins was becoming Hannibal Lecter right there at the table. Yikes!

'Yes Man' was actually based on the real events of a person who spent a year answering "yes" to any and all questions and proposals, and recording the results into a book. And true to form, Carrey also said "yes" during production. That's actually him on guitar. He also learned basic Korean, how to ride a sport bike, and he really went bungee jumping. He did have to say "no" for the body blading scene, however. Too dangerous.

ADAM SANDLER AND CO

Along for the ride. Adam Sandler is well-known for casting his friends in all his movies. This leads to some funny inside jokes. In 'Billy Madison', when Billy apologies to Danny McGrath for being mean to him in high school, Danny crosses Billy's name off his "People To Kill" list. The remaining eight on the list are actually all crew members from the film. And in 'Click', the names of the crew are on the headstones at the graveyard scene.

When 'The Waterboy' came to theatres, one of the trailers shown was for' Star Wars: Episode I - The Phantom Menace'. Many die hard Star Wars fans paid the full admission price just to watch the trailer and then left the theatre. Not Sandler fans apparently.

Getting carried away. During the dodgeball scene in 'Billy Madison', Adam Sandler was throwing at the kids as hard as he possibly could. The editor had to cut after each hit so that we don't see the children crying.

AUSTIN POWERS

According to Mike Myers, the idea for the character of Austin Powers came to him from the car radio. He was driving home one day, when Burt Bacharach's "The Look of Love" was playing. Myers began to wonder where the "swingers" of the world went to, and when he got home he started asking his then-wife if she "swung" and if he was "making her horny." And thus, 'Austin Powers: International Man of Mystery' was born.

But apparently, the word "shag" in the sequels subtitle was a little uncomfortable for some countries. Singapore changed it to, "The Spy Who Shioked Me". "Shiok" means to "treat nicely". Malaysian censors changed it to, "The Spy Who Dot-Dot-Dot Me, and some British cinemas simply put Austin Powers II on their marquees.

RANDOM FUN FACTS

1. For his role in 'Napoleon Dynamite', Jon Heder was paid only $1,000. The movie went on to gross over $40,000,000 in the United States alone. Not bad for a film that was shot in only 22 days and edited in the director's apartment on a $6,000 Macintosh with Final Cut Pro.

2. On the set of 'Home Alone', Joe Pesci deliberately avoided Macaulay Culkin because he wanted Culkin to think he was mean. And he very well might have thought so! Culkin still has a scar on his finger where Pesci bit him in one of the scenes.

3. The MPAA would not allow studio promos to include the word Fockers in their title for 'Meet The Fockers' unless they could prove there was a real family with that name living in America.

4. According to former hand model J.P. Prewitt, the fashion industry has been behind every high-profile political assassination of the last hundred years. Derek Zoolander asks "Why male models?" and after a particularly lengthy explanation from Prewitt, Zoolander responds again, "Why male models?" Ben Stiller, who plays the dimwitted male model had forgotten his line. This prompted Duchovny to ad-lib, "Are you kidding? I just told you like a minute ago."

The scene ends up reinforcing the movie's narrative of the brainless male model stereotype, and turned a mistake into one of the funniest parts of the film.

5. The coconut gag used to replicate the sound of horse hooves from 'Monty Python and the Holy Grail' came about because they couldn't afford actual horses.

6. In, 'I Love You Man', Sydney's dog is named Anwar after the former president of Egypt, Anwar Sadat. One of Sadat's daughters sued the producers of the film, because in Egyptian culture, a human compared with a dog is a serious insult.

7. The scene in '40-Year-Old Virgin' where Andy has his chest hair ripped out wasn't faked. Actor Steve Carell said, "It has to be real. It won't be as funny if it's mocked up or if it's special effect. You have to see that this is really happening." Of course, the scene had to be done in just one shot.

8. There's a moment in 'Being John Malkovich' where Malkovich gets hit in the head by a can thrown by an extra from a passing car. "Hey Malkovich! Think fast!" Neither the can nor Malkovich's genuine reaction of pain was scripted, but it was too good to not put in the movie. Instead of being fired, the extra was added to the final cut of the film and given a raise.

9. 'Trainspotting'. For the supposed worst toilet in Scotland scene, the...ahem, fecal matter was actually chocolate and apparently smelled quite delicious.

10. 'The Blues Brothers' set a world record at the time when they wrecked 103 cars during filming. This was eclipsed during the filming of 'Transformers: Dark of the Moon', where 532 cars were destroyed.

11. Life imitates art. In 'Beverly Hills Cop' the police used a fictional technology they dubbed, a "Satellite Tracking System". We now know this as GPS.

12. In 'Reservoir Dogs', Nice Guy Eddie arranges for Mr. Orange, played by Tim Roth, to be treated by a nurse he knows named Bonnie. Tarantino fans will note that in 'Pulp Fiction', Jimmy's wife is a nurse named Bonnie.

13. Harold and Kumar don't go to White Castle because the actors were big fans of the burgers. It was the only restaurant chain that would allow them to use their name for the movie!

14. Speaking of restaurants, the name of the Mexican restaurant in 'Anchor Man' translates to "We Spit In Your Food."

15. Sneaky marketing. To promote his film, and to have a laugh, I'm sure, Kevin Smith secretly joined religious groups in a protest of his own movie 'Dogma'. According to Smith, he carried a sign that read, "Dogma is dogshit" and was interviewed by a reporter who didn't know he was the writer and director of the film.

16. Apparently a lot of money was saved on special effects for the filming of 'The Mask' because Jim Carrey's body movements were so flexible and cartoonish, they didn't need

to enhance them all digitally.

17. In 'Charlie's Angels', Drew Barrymore's character tumbles down a hill, and arrives at a house with two boys playing a video game. It's the same house from 'E.T.', which Drew starred in. There's even a bowl of Reese's Pieces (E.T.'s favorite candy) and a movie poster of E.T. in the background.

18. 'Jay and Silent Bob Strike Back' was the first film that both Carrie Fisher and Mark Hamill had appeared in together since 'Return of the Jedi'. Apparently neither of them were aware of this until after shooting was completed. It would have been interesting to hear Hamill explain his role as "Cock Knocker" to Princess Leia.

19. Race is sometimes an issue. According to Will Smith, the female lead for 'Hitch' was supposed to be Caucasian, but the producers didn't want an interracial couple. Too taboo. They also didn't want the female lead to be black, as they feared it would alienate white audiences. In the end, they chose Eva Mendes, a Hispanic actress.

20. Benicio Del Toro gained 40 pounds for his role as Dr. Gonzo in 'Fear and Loathing in Las Vegas'? How'd he do it? By his own admission...eating multiple donuts every day.

TEST YOURSELF - QUESTIONS AND ANSWERS

1. The iconic red stapler coveted by Milton in 'Office Space' was what colour:

A) Blue

B) Red

C) Yellow

2. Neil Patrick Harris' career was relaunched by which movie:

A) Glee

B) Harold and Kumar Go to White Castle

C) How I Met Your Mother

3. Derek and Hansel settle their dispute in 'Zoolander' by competing in a:

A) Face off

B) Pose-A-Thon

C) Walk off

4. Which infamous athlete has a pivotal cameo in 'Dodgeball: A True Underdog Story'?

A) John McEnroe

B) Lance Armstrong

C) Mike Tyson

5. This Owen Wilson and Vince Vaughn film used 100 real Google employees as extras:

A) The Wedding Crashers

B) The Internship

C) Starsky and Hutch

ANSWERS

1. B
2. C
3. C
4. B
5. B

CHAPTER SIX

THINGS TAKE
A DRAMATIC TURN

Dramatic movies draw us in. They tell us stories of struggle and challenge, and portray deeply developed characters. They make us laugh a little, and sometimes cry. And they almost always encourage us to think about life in ways we'd not done before. Explore the rich detail and interesting facts from these cinematic powerhouses.

GANGS OF NEW YORK

Dragged out of obscurity. Apparently Daniel Day-Lewis was happily living his life in Italy as a cobbler's apprentice, when Martin Scorsese and Leonardo DiCaprio convinced him to take the role of Bob the Butcher for 'Gangs of New York'. And once he accepted, he threw himself into the role in typical Daniel Day-Lewis fashion.

To simulate Bill's glass eye, he had his own covered in prosthetic glass and learned how to tap it with the tip of his knife. Without blinking. This is something he improvised himself for the film, much to the delight of the crew. He refused to break character as normal, speaking with his accent during the entire production, even on the last day when filming wrapped.

Apparently one waitress was afraid to go near him, and he had several scuffles in Roman parking lots.

He also hired two circus performers to teach him how to throw daggers, and he worked in a butcher's shop for several weeks to learn how to properly and meticulously carve carcasses like a professional. Day-Lewis stayed in form even when Leonardo DiCaprio accidentally broke his nose during a fight scene.

The gangs that were featured in the film are based on actual historical gangs from the Five Points. Although "The Dead Rabbits" require a bit of history for it to make sense to modern viewers. Back then, the word "dead" was actually a variation for "very", and "rabbit" is a phonetic corruption of the Gaelic word "ráibéad", which means "man to be feared". Therefore, Dead Ráibéad meant: A man to be greatly feared.

THE WOLF OF WALL STREET

Apparently, Leonardo DiCaprio has never done drugs in his life, so he had to consult with drug experts for the role of Jordan Belfort. His character was in a constant drug-induced high, whether it was crack, cocaine, or alcohol, so he and Jonah Hill watched videos of the drunkest man in the world for extra inspiration.

When it came time to snort lines of cocaine for the scenes, the actors actually used crushed B vitamins. Jonah claims that he got sick with bronchitis after so much inhaling and had to be hospitalized. The real Jordan Belfort was also on set to coach DiCaprio on his behavior, especially instructing him in the various ways he had reacted to Quaaludes.

All of Matthew McConaughey's scenes were shot on the second week of filming. The chest beating and humming ritual we see was actually improvised, and is something he often does to prepare before the cameras start to roll. At the lunch scene, that brief shot of DiCaprio looking away uneasily is actually him looking to director Martin Scorsese for approval to continue. This take was the one used in the film, after DiCaprio encouraged them to include it. He later claimed, "it set the tone" for the rest of the film.

The F-bomb and its numerous conjugations are said 569 times in the movie, making this the film with the most uses of the word in a main-stream, R-Rated, non-documentary film.

EYES WIDE SHUT

In it for the long haul. Both Tom Cruise and Nicole Kidman signed open-ended contracts for their roles in the film. Director Stanley Kubrick was famous for very long shoots, so they agreed to work on this project until Kubrick released them from it, however long that may be. Vincent D'Onofrio, who had worked with Kubrick for 'Full Metal Jacket', advised them to "rent a house or apartment, because you're going to be in England for a while."

And it's a good thing they did. The film is in the Guinness Book for longest constant movie shoot at 400 days. If you can believe it, it took 95 takes before Kubrick was happy with how Tom Cruise walked through the front door.

Some viewers didn't seem to understand why Nicole Kidman's performance seemed so "dreamy". They must not have been aware that the movie is based on a novella from the 1920s titled, "Dream Story". The effect is intentional.

Kubrick died just a week after screening his final cut to studio executives, fuelling more conspiracy theories, as the film showed behind-the-scenes strange behaviours of the wealthy elite of society.

THE DEER HUNTER

There are many famous scenes to discuss from this classic film. One in particular almost caused Robert De Niro to leave the production. Apparently, director Michael Cimino convinced Christopher Walken to spit in De Niro's face during one of the Russian Roulette scenes. De Niro was in complete shock, furious, and nearly left the set. Cimino later said of Walken, "He's got courage!"

A piece of unintentional footage was caught on film when the group were being held prisoner over the river. When John Savage is yelling, "Michael, there's rats in here, Michael", while he is stuck in the cage in the river, he was actually yelling at the director, not De Niro's character, also named Michael. There is real panic in his voice because of his fear of the rats which had infested the river zone. The rats were real, the mosquitoes were real, and they were actually tied up in bamboo cages along the River Kwai.

The woman in charge of casting the extras in Thailand had a difficult time finding a vicious-looking local who was up for the task of slapping De Niro in the face. She eventually found someone who had a strong distaste for Americans. And this time it was De Niro's turn. He suggested that Christopher Walken be slapped by one of the guards without warning, catching a very genuine reaction.

THE TRUMAN SHOW

Would you be surprised to know that actors Ed Harris and Jim Carrey never actually met during filming. It's true.

And you might remember the promotional poster which featured Jim Carrey's face comprised of hundreds of individual images from the film. It was created by artist Rob Silverman for a rumoured cost of $75,000.

When Siskel and Ebert reviewed the film on their show, they gave it two enthusiastic thumbs up. They also gave a public apology to Jim Carrey for saying he would never have a career after 'Ace Ventura'. Interestingly enough, it was Jim's performance in 'Ace Ventura' that inspired director Peter Weir to cast him as the role of Truman. He said it reminded him of Charlie Chaplin.

Carrey remarked that he was able to relate to Truman because he is constantly being watched by fans and paparazzi where ever he goes.

After the film was released, a psychiatrist shared that he had five schizophrenic patients, and had heard of another dozen, who believed their lives were reality television shows just like Truman's. Apparently, one patient climbed the Statue of Liberty in New York, believing that this was the key to reuniting with his high school girlfriend who would be waiting at the top.

THE CURIOUS CASE OF BENJAMIN BUTTON

The movie is based on a short story by F. Scott Fitzgerald, about a man born in his seventies and ages backwards. And the story is based on a remark by author Mark Twain, who famously said that "the best part of life was from the beginning and the worst part was the end."

Like many of the more visually interesting performance we have seen, the makeup department had a large role to play. For his role as Benjamin, who was aging backwards, Brad Pitt sat for 5 hours each day to complete the make-up required for the role.

To add an extra level of authenticity, the filmmakers worked closely with Levi's clothing company, obtaining items from their Vintage collection to match the various time periods captured throughout the film.

This wasn't the first time director David Fincher had worked with Brad Pitt. They had previously teamed up for 'Fight Club', and when Benjamin's father asks about "the house on Paper Street" it's a nod to the house where Tyler Durden planned his revolution.

NO COUNTRY FOR OLD MEN

Two days after winning the lead role, actor Josh Brolin badly injured his shoulder in a motorcycle accident. He said in an interview, that as he was flying through the air and over the car that hit him, all he could think about was that he wouldn't be able to work with the Coen brothers. It turned out to be a non-issue as his character is shot in the shoulder at the beginning of the film.

Remember the scene when Brolin's character Moss is lying hurt on the ground, after crossing the border? That's when a mariachi group starts singing to him. In case you don't speak Spanish, the words translate to: "You wanted to fly without wings, you wanted to touch the sky, you wanted too much wealth, you wanted to play with fire". Pretty much sums up the entire movie in that one song!

Joel Coen and Ethan Coen had to convince Javier Bardem to take the role of Anton Chigurh. They used an old photo from a brothel patron taken in 1979 as a model for his hair style. When he first saw his new haircut, Bardem said, "Oh no, now I won't get laid for the next two months". This prompted a happy high-five from the brothers, as they knew that meant he would look as creepy as they'd hoped. He did.

The movie has been described differently by the people involved. Tommy Lee Jones has said that "the movie is both a horror and a comedy"; Kelly Macdonald says, "it's simply a Coen Bothers film and that they are their own genre"; and Ethan Coen said, "it's as close as we'll ever come to an action movie."

THE PEOPLE VS. LARRY FLINT

Saved by a film. Director Milos Forman claims Courtney Love was under the influence of drugs when she came to audition for the role of Althea. He nearly dismissed her immediately, but quickly realized she was perfect for the role...on one condition. Love had to promise to stay clean and have regular drug tests throughout production. She agreed, and credits Forman's influence for helping her win her battle against drug addiction and re-kindle her career.

That didn't keep her out of trouble though. She was arrested several times for wearing scandalous and revealing costumes in public. During filming of a jail scene, she was mistaken for a convicted criminal and was handcuffed and taken to booking by one of the officers.

The real Larry Flynt was denied an invitation to the 1997 Academy Awards, so Woody Harrelson, who played him in the movie, snuck him in as his "+1".

APOCALYPTO

You'll have to look closely, but Mel Gibson included a "Where's Waldo" joke in the film. Watch the scene where Jaguar Paw stumbles into the pit of bodies after the ritual sacrifice. Gibson inserted a single frame of a man dressed as Waldo.

Despite that one occurrence, Gibson was very attentive to historical details and the entirety of the film was spoken in the Yucatec Mayan language. Many of the actors had to study and learn the language for the film. And the stretched earlobes? Those were all custom-made silicon prostheses.

For the waterfall jump scene, actor Rudy Youngblood jumped from a 15-story building in Veracruz using a harness. 10 takes in all. The shot was then digitally superimposed over the real waterfall. Director Mel Gibson had apparently harassed Youngblood about his initial fear of jumping, so Youngblood got together with the stunt crew and goaded Gibson into taking a jump himself.

Apparently, a cow that was trying to cross upstream went over the 170 foot falls. It emerged at the bottom alive but dazed. It had banged its head on rocks near the bank. A local man swam over to calm the cow down and shortly after, it climbed up on the river bank and began eating grass as if nothing had happened.

12 YEARS A SLAVE

Emotionally charged. To prepare for the more brutal scenes they had to film together, Michael Fassbender and Lupita Nyong'o had a ritual they called, "making nice." They would grasp hands and look each other in the eye. This helped them to endure the intensity they had to summon for their performances as slave master and slave.

Fassbender also had his makeup artist paint alcohol into his moustache so he would smell like an alcoholic to the other actors. The idea was they would then respond naturally to the smell and offer a more convincing reaction to his behaviour.

In one gruesome detail, the tree where Solomon witnesses several men being lynched was actually used for lynching during the Slave Era. It is surrounded by the graves of many murdered slaves.

Four years after Solomon Northup was freed from bondage, he disappeared and no one knows what became of him.

BOYHOOD

Richard Linklater shot the movie 'Boyhood' over the course of 12 years. There were only a total of 45 days of filming, but it followed one boy and his family from childhood all the way to college. It was essentially a collection of smaller films edited into one larger one. Had Linklater died during the 12-year shoot, it was agreed Ethan Hawke would take over duty as director to finish the project.

To keep things authentic, Linklater asked Patricia Arquette, who played the boy's mom, not to have any plastic surgeries, as it wouldn't make sense for her character.

Linklater's next film, 'Everybody Wants Some!' is meant to be the continuation of 'Boyhood', picking up in college where the main character meets his new roommates and his first girlfriend.

THERE WILL BE BLOOD

You might think twice about your dinner choice. According to director Paul Thomas Anderson, the fake oil used throughout the movie included "the stuff they put in chocolate milkshakes at McDonald's."

And speaking of milkshakes, the infamous "I drink your milkshake" line is more or less a real-life quote, not one of Day-Lewis' legendary improvs this time. But he did improvise the entire speech to the townsfolk of Little Boston. Everything from bringing schools and bread to the town was completely ad-libbed and unscripted.

Knowing of Daniel Day-Lewis' penchant for method acting, director Paul Thomas Anderson's long-time costume designer gave Day-Lewis three hats to choose from for his role as Daniel Plainview. The actor spent time with them all before deciding on his preference. According to Anderson, "you knew he was Daniel Plainview once the hat went on. And by the way, the sweat stains are real."

FURY

Pushing the limits. Director David Ayer employed some peculiar techniques to get the tank crew to bond together. He had them abuse each other verbally and physically, and made them fight each other on set before shooting their scenes. The actors had a confidentiality agreement not to disclose certain things said and done during production. Logan Lerman has stated that the experience "left scars I'm healing from."

Apparently, Shia LaBeouf pulled out his own tooth in the first few weeks of filming and flat out refused to shower...for four months. He wanted to "better understand how his character would have felt living in the trenches", and no one could convince him otherwise. The solution was to put him in his own hotel, apart from the rest of the cast and crew.

It wasn't explicitly stated, but it's likely that Brad Pitt's character Wardaddy was a WWI veteran. To start, he is much older than the average WWII NCO (non-commissioned officer), who likely would have been in his mid 20s to early 30s. Pitt was 50. His long service record is also mentioned in the film, and being a WWI veteran would explain why his character spoke German before the war had started.

If you look closely, you can see a picture of a woman's face on the grips of his revolver. These were called "sweetheart" grips. They were made by removing the government-issue grips and replacing them with custom-made ones from scrounged Plexiglas. They'd put a picture of a wife or lover, their "sweetheart" underneath the glass.

CASTAWAY

Before filming began, several crew members camped on the island to practice survival skills and gather the details needed to help develop Tom Hanks' character Chuck. They had trouble lighting a fire, catching fish, and opening a coconut. These were all situations that became scenes for the movie. They also talked with a volleyball and gathered packages that had washed up on the beach. This is the inspiration for Wilson, his volleyball companion. In fact, actual lines of dialogue were written for Wilson, to create a more natural flow of interaction with the inanimate co-star.

To make the character come across as an average out of shape middle-aged man, Hanks gained weight for the role and stopped exercising altogether. Then, to prepare for the deserted island scenes, production was halted for an entire year so Hanks could lose 50 pounds and grow out his hair.

If you want to check out the island that 'Cast Away' was filmed on, put -17.609277,177.0397 into Google Maps. The beach where Hanks writes HELP is the eastern most part of Monuriki, Fiji.

RANDOM FUN FACTS

1. The slightest change. According to Ben Affleck, director David Fincher, is the only director he's met "who can do everybody else's job better than they could." He tested the theory on the set of 'Gone Girl', by changing the lens setting on a camera by an almost indiscernible amount. He made a wager that Fincher wouldn't notice, but lost the bet when Fincher asked, "Why does the camera look a little dim?"

2. The magic was real. In order to avoid CGI and the need to fake the magical illusions seen in 'The Illusionist', actor Ed Norton received intensive training in sleight of hand techniques from established magicians. So what you see is Norton really performing the tricks.

3. "You talking to me?" The famous line from Taxi Driver, in fact that whole scene, was improvised by Robert De Niro. The script simply said, "Travis talks to himself in the mirror".

4. The opening weigh-in scene for 'Ali' took much longer to shoot than anticipated, and went hours past midnight. So actor Jon Voight was taking extras' cell phones and calling their homes on their behalf. The message for more than a few voice-mails went, "This is Jon Voight, don't worry, your husband is still on set working, not out in a bar, or chasing

girls."

5. Harsh filming conditions. According to Leonardo DiCaprio, the only time they halted filming of 'The Revenant' was when conditions were so extreme that the camera actually froze and they couldn't stop their teeth from clacking together.

6. 'Leaving Las Vegas'. To prepare for his role as an alcoholic drinking himself to death, Nicolas Cage would binge drink and film himself while drunk. That way he could study his speech patterns. Although he allegedly took magic mushrooms with his cat, there is no evidence he used inspiration from this experience for the role.

7. Allegedly, the actual mafia didn't allow producers of 'The Godfather' to use the word Mafia in the movie. In one story, they went so far as to send "family" members to monitor filming.

8. The lineup scene in 'The Usual Suspects' was originally scripted to be a serious one, but the actors couldn't stop laughing. Benicio del Toro kept farting throughout, and when it came time for him to deliver the line, "Give me the keys, you f*cking c*cksucker!" the ad-libbed response from the cop "In English please?" had them all laughing even harder. So they kept it in.

9. In preparation for his role as the stoic driver in 'Drive', actor Ryan Gosling completely restored a 1973 Chevy Malibu. The same car his character uses in the film.

10. That cat Marlon Brando is stroking as godfather Vito Corleone? Apparently, that was a stray that was found on set. Coppola dropped it on his lap for the scene where he is dishing out his ruling on a man's punishment.

11. In the film, 'The Wrestler', actor Mickey Rourke actually "blades" himself, by making a small cut on his forehead with a razor blade. This is also known in the wrestling world as, "getting color". Wrestlers do it to add bloody realism to their other-wise scripted performances in the ring.

12. Will Smith's character in 'The Pursuit of Happiness' had to be able to solve a Rubik's Cube in under two minutes, so Speedcubing champions were hired to coach him how to do it.

13. As part of their training for 'End of Watch, Jake Gyllenhaal and Michael Peña got a little too close to the action. They spent five months doing 12-hour ride-alongs with on-duty LAPD officers, and on Gyllenhaal's first time, he actually witnessed a murder.

14. The Russian translations of some Hollywood titles are rather humorous. 'Silver Linings Playbook' became, 'My Boyfriend Is a Psycho', 'Big Miracle' is 'Everybody Loves Whales', 'A Walk to Remember' is 'Hurry Up and Fall in Love', and 'Lawless' is the 'Drunkest Country in the World'.

15. Marlon Brando wanted to make Don Corleone "look like a bulldog," so he stuffed his cheeks with cotton for his audition. Coppola loved the effect and had a mouthpiece

made for the actual filming.

16. Movie making can be long and tiring work. Especially if you are writing, producing and starring. While filming 'Good Will Hunting', Matt Damon actually fell asleep in Minnie Driver's bed on the set of her college dorm. They let him continue to sleep and started filming the scene from above. The dopey mumbles we see in the final film are real.

17. Jonah Hill had big crazy teeth for his role as Donnie in 'The Wolf of Wall Street'. At first, they caused an audible lisp, so he spent over two hours on the phone calling random businesses to get rid of it.

18. If you look closely during 'Money ball', when Brad Pitt's character is having a conversation with his ex-wife and her partner, there is a book called, "By the Sea" on the side table. Pitt ended up starring in the movie by the same name a few years later.

19. During a meeting with the real Dr. Michael Burry for the movie 'The Big Short', Christian Bale asked if he could have his cargo shorts and T-shirt to wear in the movie. He did!

20. It was in his genes! Al Pacino's maternal grandparents actually immigrated to America from Italy. From Corleone, Sicily to be exact. Just as Vito Corleone did in the Godfather series.

TEST YOURSELF - QUESTIONS AND ANSWERS

1. The last movie to be released on VHS was:

A) A History of Violence

B) Sin City

C) The War of the Worlds

2. The password for the mansion party in 'Eyes Wide Shut' was:

A) Fraternity

B) Fidelio

C) Fidelity

3. For a party scene in 'Almost Famous', character Russell Hammond cries out, "I am a golden god!" when he is on acid. That is a reference to which legendary rocker who is purported to have said the same thing from his Hollywood balcony?

A) Jim Morrison

B) Jimi Hendrix

C) Robert Plant

4. Actor Josh Brolin was welcomed by the gay community, and praised for portraying "The most hated man in San Francisco's history" in which film?

A) Philadelphia

B) Milk

C) Brokeback Mountain

5. The first woman to win the Academy Award for best director was Kathryn Bigelow. It was for which film?

A) Slumdog Millionaire

B) The Hurt Locker

C) Vicky Christina Barcelona

ANSWERS

1. A
2. B
3. C
4. B
5. B

CHAPTER SEVEN

BITS & BITES

There are thousands of movies and thousands of actors who star in them. With that much going on, there are bound to have been some odd and strange occurrences. From intense commitment to the method acting style, to ingenious and innovative filming techniques, enjoy this collection of random and assorted interesting facts!

WHAT'S WITH THE TEETH?

During the filming of 'Fight Club', Brad Pitt chipped a tooth, but he left it that way in order to make his character seem more authentic. Jim Carrey went for a similar effect and had a dental cap removed for 'Dumb and Dumber'. For 'The Hangover', Ed Helms took out a fake front tooth and they worked it into the script. His character was a dentist, and while under the influence of various substances, he pulled it out himself.

Johnny Depp's Captain Jack character from 'Pirates of the Caribbean' has quite a few gold teeth in the film. That was Depp's idea. But he predicted studio executives would want fewer gold teeth than the look he was going for, so he told his dentist to implant extra that he could use as a bargaining tool. In the end,

Captain Sparrow got just the amount of gold Depp had envisioned.

Viggo Mortensen also chipped a tooth while filming a fight sequence for 'Lord of the Rings'. He wanted director Peter Jackson to just superglue it back on so he could finish the scene, but despite his protests, he was taken to the dentist instead.

A couple of actors even opted to have their dentist literally grind their teeth down for a role. Robert De Niro did this for 'Cape Fear', allegedly paying his dentist $5000 to deform his teeth and make him look extra creepy. Jaime Foxx got the same treatment for his role as a homeless musical genius in 'The Soloist'. According to Foxx, "I wanted to break up my big shining piano keys to give them a little character."

METHOD ACTING MADNESS

Method acting usually involves actors identifying with their characters as closely as they possibly can. Think Daniel Day-Lewis...in any role he's ever had. Many actors today still pay homage to Marlon Brando as their personal inspiration for their own versions of method acting. As one story goes, while Brando was taking classes to be an actor, the class was instructed to act like chickens...with the added twist that a nuclear bomb was about to fall on them. Most of the class clucked like chickens about to die a horrible death and ran wildly around the room. But not Brando. He sat calmly and pretended to lay an egg. When asked why he had chosen this reaction, Brando replied, "I'm a chicken, what do I know about bombs?"

Sometimes actors get so into their roles, you could say they lose a little bit of objectivity. At least so it seems when we read of the stories from the set. While playing his crazed and twisted version of the Joker in 'The Suicide Squad', apparently Jared Leto stayed in character on and off camera. Some of his antics included harassing his co-stars Joker-style and sending them strange packages containing items like bullets, a dead pig, a live rat, anal beads and used condoms.

During the filming of 'The Deer Hunter', John Cazale was dying of lung cancer and passed away shortly thereafter. As well as playing a role in the same film, Meryl Streep was also living with Cazale as he went through his illness. Legend has it that Dustin Hoffman encouraged the producers of 'Kramer vs. Kramer' to get Streep for the movie, which began filming shortly after Cazale's death. Hoffman wanted to capture her genuine grief so that she would come across authentically vulnerable on-screen. To capitalize on her emotional turmoil and pain, he reportedly would slap her off-camera and taunt her about Cazale. The role launched her career and got her an Academy Award, but only she knows if it was worth the hardships during filming.

To get himself fully immersed into the mindset of a serial killer for his role in 'The Fall', actor Jamie Dornan actually stalked a woman in real life. Thankfully she didn't notice.

Slightly less edgy, but interesting nonetheless, James Franco actually lived on the streets of L.A., begging for change to live and sleeping on the pavement. This was all to prepare for his role as Robert De Niro's drug-addicted, homeless son in 'City By The

Sea'. "It's not so hard", he said, claiming to have made $20 in 30 minutes with a sign that said, "Homeless, please help".

STRANGE INSPIRATION

When animators first started preparing the character of Aladdin, they used Michael J. Fox for inspiration. But they weren't happy with the end result, as Aladdin came out a little too cute, so they turned to Tom Cruise instead. Animators studied his films and transferred Cruise's confidence into Aladdin's attitude and poses. The idea was to make him the kind of guy Jasmine would risk everything to be with.

This wasn't the first time Tom Cruise inspired a movie character. Apparently Christian Bale did the same, but in a far less flattering way. For his role in 'American Psycho', Bale channelled Cruise after seeing him in a late-night interview. According to Bale, Cruise "had an insane friendliness with nothing behind the eyes." Just the right look for a soulless psychopath I guess. Yikes!

He might deny the comparison, but nobody's buying it. Anyone who has had any interactions with Lorne Michaels or seen him speak, knows he is definitely the inspiration for Mike Myers' Dr Evil. There's one scene in 'Austin Powers', where Dr. Evil freaks out when he's told he won't be getting the laser-beam-wielding sharks he demanded. According to one anonymous Saturday Night Live actor, "I've seen that conversation between Lorne and the set designer 500 times at 10:30 on Saturday night." And apparently, Michaels unconsciously "ends everything by bringing his pinkie up and chewing the fingernail." Just like Dr. Evil.

Michael Fassbender worked hard to create a believable performance for his role as David, the android in 'Prometheus'. For inspiration, he looked to David Bowie, as well as one other source that might be a little harder to pick up on. According to Fassbender, he was inspired by famed Olympic diver Greg Louganis. He said, "When you read a script, certain images or names pop up, and for some reason Greg Louganis came up. I knew I wanted to have good posture and a sort of economy of movement." In particular, Fassbender was mesmerized by the way Louganis would walk out onto the diving board. The measured and stiff-armed steps gave him the idea for how David would move.

COSTUMES SO GOOD THEY HURT

I bet you thought Michel Pfeiffer's Cat Woman suit was pretty tight, right? Well it was. In fact, it was vacuum sealed. It was so tight, in fact, that she could only wear it for limited amounts of time to avoid passing out. And she couldn't hear her own voice properly as the costume restricted the air flow in her lungs.

Jim Carrey had a bit of a rough go with one of his confining costumes also. Enduring his role as the Grinch was so challenging that he actually sought counselling by a US Navy Seal on torture resistance techniques. In total, Carrey spent 92 days in full Grinch makeup. It took 2.5 hours each morning to put it on, and an hour to get it off. This was plenty long enough for him to become, in his own words, "a Zen master".

In a gesture of empathy, director Ron Howard had the makeup

applied on himself. This angered Carrey at first, as he thought they had hired a stunt double who looked nothing like him. Howard ended up directing an entire day's shooting with the costume on.

BEFORE THEY WERE FAMOUS

It's not all glamour all the time. Many actors have struggled until they got their big break. Here are just a few stories:

Brad Pitt's first job in Hollywood was as a dancing promotional chicken for an El Pollo Loco restaurant on Sunset Boulevard. He was living in his car at the time. Matt Damon was a sidewalk break-dancer, and Johnny Depp sold pens over the phone. Channing Tatum was a male-stripper, so his role in 'Magic Mike' came pretty easily to him.

Hugh Jackman worked as a party clown. Apparently, he made $50 per show. Rachel McAdams was a McDonald's employee for three years, and Amy Adams was a Hooters girl. Vince Vaughn made his living as a lifeguard at the YMCA, while actress Eva Mendes sold hot dogs on sticks in a shopping mall.

QUIET ON THE SET!

Different directors have taken a variety of measures to keep order on the set. During the production of 'Snatch', director Guy Ritchie enforced a unique system of fines. There were fines for mobile phones ringing on set, for arriving late, for taking naps during shooting, and for being "cheeky", "unfunny", or "moaning and complaining". Apparently, one crew was even fined for allowing the set to run out of coffee cups.

James Cameron has been known to be quite ruthless when it comes to cell phones on his sets. During the filming of 'Avatar', he was known to keep a nail gun on hand, which he used to nail ringing phones to the wall above the exit sign. Quentin Tarantino is anti-cell phone as well. He has a strict rule against them, and cast and crew actually have to sign an agreement contract that they won't bring them around his cameras. As Tarantino puts it, "We actually have a Checkpoint Charlie" and as you enter the set, there is a designated person who collects them.

Language can sometimes be an issue too. During 'The Hunger Games' production, a swear jar was kept on set and allegedly more than half of it was contributed by Jennifer Lawrence. She should get together with James McAvoy, who was the worst offender on the set of 'The Chronicles of Narnia'. His swearing was allegedly, "out of hand" so they too had to enforce a swear jar.

WHAT ARE THEY SMOKING?

Actors are often depicted smoking in films, but things aren't always quite what they seem. You may have noticed Sigourney Weaver's character smoking in 'Avatar'. Well, there wasn't actually anything there in reality. It was a CGI cigarette. And the boys in 'Stand By Me' were all smoking cabbage for their scenes. It might seem like Kevin Spacey and Wes Bentley are under the effects of the wacky tabacky that they are smoking in 'American

Beauty', but they were actually smoking honey tobacco.

Natalie Portman was quite young when she appeared in Luc Besson's, 'Leon', and her parents were extremely worried about the smoking scenes in the film. So they all came together and created a special contract for her performance. Accordingly, there could only be five smoking scenes in the film, Portman would never be seen to inhale or exhale smoke, and her character Mathilda would give up the habit at some point in the film. If you pay attention, you'll see that all of these mandates were adhered to.

TINSEL TOWN

Here's a few facts about the city of Hollywood that you might not know about:

Actors aren't given a star on the walk of fame, they actually have to pay for it. $30,000 to be precise. And there's one star that isn't on the sidewalk. Muhammad Ali didn't want to be walked on, so his is on the wall of the Kodak Theatre instead.

Did you know there's only one species of frog in the world that actually makes a "ribbit" sound? But it has become the accepted frog noise around the world because that species resides in Hollywood and was used for sound effects in many films.

And frogs aren't the only animals living in Hollywood. Apparently, there's a population of wild chickens living under a freeway. They've been there since the 1970s, and no one knows how they got there.

The famous sign in the Hollywood hills has been there awhile too. Since 1923 actually. It was put up by a real estate agent and originally spelled out HOLLYWOODLAND. It used to be lit up by light bulbs and the guy who changed them when they burned out lived in a cabin close-by.

DOING HONOUR TO IMPROV

There are many movies that contain lines and scenes that weren't scripted and were totally improvised by the actors. We've noted just a small amount here in the pages of this book. 'Good Will Hunting' is one such film, which should be no surprise really, considering Robin Williams starred in it. So to give the skill of improv its due and honor, Matt Damon and Ben Affleck, who had written the script, printed it out during awards season so people could read along as they watched the film. This let people see exactly where the actors deviated from the script into improv, to get a better sense of how the movie came together. By the way, the pair won the Academy Award for best original screenplay.

DANGER ON SET

Remember when the Nazi cinema was on fire during 'Inglorious Basterds'? Well, it really *was* on fire, and things got a little out of hand. Actor Eli Roth was actually hospitalized for the burns he received, and the set nearly collapsed.

Linda Hamilton got a bit carried away on the set of 'Terminator 2'. While filming the scenes in the mental hospital, she requested the actors playing orderlies to actually physically strike her with their night sticks. But they wouldn't comply, because they didn't want to hit a woman, so she showed them how to do it during her escape scene. What we see on the screen is actually her hitting him in the face with the club!

And the infamous car chase scene for 'The French Connection' was done completely illegally. With speeds up to 90 mph, it's no surprise there were real accidents with civilian drivers. One unlucky guy drove into the shot and was t-boned!

Stanley Kubrick once used insecticide to mimic fog, and the cast of 'Fear and Desire' were literally breathing it in. In 'A Clockwork Orange', another Kubrick film, Malcolm McDowell was actually enduring real torture. He has recounted how he got a blood clot under his rib from the scene that called for a boot heel to be driven into his chest. And the metal devices used to hold his eyes open were actually scratching his eyes!

WHAT DO THEY DO WITH ALL THAT MONEY?

It's no secret that actors get paid pretty well for what they do. And some of them spend it on unique and interesting collections. Johnny Depp likes to collect insects, animal skeletons and rare books. But that's not his only pursuit. Apparently, Depp has hundreds of Barbie Dolls as well, including special editions based on celebrities. He says he uses them to test out different voices for his characters.

Does it surprise you to know that Angelina Jolie has an extensive collection of knives? She's been collecting them since her mother gave her one when she was 12. And when retro lunchboxes became too expensive, Quentin Tarantino started collecting TV show themed board games instead. We're told his favourite is a game called, Universe, which is based on Stanley Kubrick's '2001: A Space Odyssey'.

Tom Hanks likes old typewriters and has over 50 of them, and Penelope Cruz has a penchant for clothes hangers to go with her vast collection of designer clothing. She's got over 500. Ben Stiller goes for anything Star Trek related, with his prize possession being a pair of Spock ears signed by Leonard Nimoy. And last but not least, Amanda Seyfried likes to collect taxidermy animals. She says it's much easier to have stuffed creatures over the real thing when you live in the city. Her collection includes a horse, a miniature zebra, an owl, a goat, a fox and a deer. Apparently, they all have names too.

OFF CAMERA ANTICS

The average movie takes only a couple months to shoot, and actors aren't always needed on set for the entire duration. So what are they doing in their free time? Quite a few of them are into the gaming world. Actress Mila Kunis became so addicted to the World of Warcraft that she had to force herself to stop playing. She'd also started using a different voice as people quickly recognized who her game character was. Leonardo DiCaprio is apparently also a bit of an addict...to his PlayStation, and Nicole Kidman is in love with her Nintendo. Steve Carell is into another kind of game...online poker. He jokes that "most of the money I've earned has been spent online."

David Arquette attempted a second career as a 'professional' wrestler, and even won the World Heavyweight Championship. His win has been cited as the reason for the demise of the promotion. But that's not the strangest thing David has going for him. His real hobby is knitting! He's appeared on the cover of "Celebrity Scarves 2: Hollywood Knits for Breast Cancer Research".

STRANGE DIETS

There are many vegetarians and vegans running around Hollywood, from Natalie Portman to Woody Harrelson. Leonardo DiCaprio is a vegetarian, but he gave that up for a moment on the set of 'The Revenant'. Concerned that the jelly bison liver that the props department had made didn't look genuine enough, DiCaprio opted on eating the real thing instead. After it was cleared by his lawyers and agents, Leo bit in and had this to say: "The bad part is the membrane around it. It's like a balloon. When you bite into it, it bursts in your mouth." He also said he'd never do that again.

He should have taken a word of advice from Jules in 'Pulp Fiction'..."Sewer rat may taste like pumpkin pie, but I'd never know, 'cause I'd never eat the filthy muthaf**ka. Samuel Jackson is a vegetarian in real life too. Ashton Kutcher took it to the next level for his role as Steve Jobs. He mimicked Jobs' fruitarian diet but didn't do it correctly and was briefly hospitalized for pancreatic pain.

Heard of the Marilyn Monroe diet? Apparently, she started her day with two raw eggs whipped in warm milk. She'd then skip lunch, and would eat a huge dinner of boiled liver, steak or lamb and five carrots. Desert was a hot-fudge sundae.

LYING TO GET THE PART

Did you know that there was an era in history where actors were considered to be professional liars, and so were denied a Christian burial? And some actors want a role so bad they're willing to lie to get it. Both Mila Kunis and Laurence Fishburne claimed they were older than their 14 years to get the parts they were after. Mila for 'That 70's Show' and Laurence, who was Larry at the time, for 'Apocalypse Now'.

Robert Pattinson lied about his acting experience in order to star in 'Harry Potter'. Unemployed at the time, Pattinson told casting directors that he had attended Oxford and The Royal Academy of Dramatic Arts.

Liam Hemsworth lied about his experience too. To secure a role in 'Last Song', he embellished upon his skills as an experienced volleyball player. It soon became apparent that he had virtually no experience in the sport, so the directors had to get the extras to lose to Hemsworth on purpose so they wouldn't make him look so bad on film.

Rachel McAdams was desperate to star in 'To The Wonder', despite an allergy to horses, and a fear of them too. Her character interacts with over 50 horses in the film! But she left those details out and got the part.

WHAT'S THAT SOUND?

Most film productions are split into different departments, each with its own role to play. Here's some examples of innovation and creativity from the Sound Department:

For the boxing scenes in 'Raging Bull', when punches are landing, we're really hearing the sounds of melons and tomatoes being squashed. And the sound of camera flashes going off in the crowd were actually gun shots. The sound tech for the movie deliberately destroyed the recordings so they couldn't be used again in future films.

The fight scenes in 'Indiana Jones' don't feature the effects real bodies being hit with punches either. The sounds are made from hitting a pile of leather jackets with a baseball bat.

And speaking of vegetables...remember the alien language from 'District 9'? That comes from the sound of rubbing pumpkins together.

The iconic percussion beats from the 'Terminator' theme? That's not a synthesizer. It's the sound tech striking a cast-iron frying pan.

For the shrieking sound of the giant spider Shelob in 'Lord of the Rings', crew used a combination of several sounds. These included a plastic alien toy, hissing steam, and the shriek of a Tasmanian Devil.

When 'Star Wars' first came out, kids everywhere mimicked the sound of lightsabers. Little did they know, the effect is a combination of the hum of an idling 35mm movie projector with the feedback sound caused by passing a stripped microphone cable past a television set.

Also from space...the sound we hear when the automatic doors open on the USS Enterprise in 'Star Trek' is actually a Russian train's toilet flushing!

RANDOM FUN FACTS

1. Ever wonder how they make the creepy decomposing faces of the cursed pirates in 'Pirates of the Caribbean'? It's turkey jerky scanned into the computer!

2. While filming 'American Honey', the cast went on a tattoo bender getting tattoos in every town they stopped in. That's how Shia LaBeouf came to have several 1990s rapper tattoos across his knees.

3. Whenever anyone is in a room with a dead person in 'The Sixth Sense', their breath becomes visible. This isn't CGI. Production actually built a cold room where they could drop to freezing temperatures in just under 12 minutes.

4. In a coincidence almost too hard to believe, Sean Connery was once stopped for speeding by Sergeant James Bond.

5. Lauren Bacall trained her voice to go deeper by reading aloud in lower tones until it became her actual new voice.

6. No more visits to China for Brad. For his role in 'Seven Years in Tibet', Brad Pitt is banned from ever entering China. He shouldn't feel to bad, the government also won't allow movies involving time travel. Sorry Bill and Ted.

7. Those screams were real! For the bedroom scene in 'The Godfather', a real horse head was used from a dog food

factory. The actor wan't told the plastic prop had been replaced with the real thing!

8. When directing, Clint Eastwood is known to simply say "okay" instead of "action" and "cut." Apparently, the directors from his western days were often very loud and their voices would spook the horses.

9. In 'Dances with Wolves', during the scene where a buffalo is charging at the young Sioux, Smiles A-Lot, the buffalo is actually running towards a pile of Oreo cookies. Apparently they're its favourite treat!

10. In less than 3 years, the famous scene of Keanu Reeves dodging bullets in 'The Matrix' had been spoofed in over 20 different movies.

11. Do they go too far? Apparently, The Humane Society objected to the scene in the 'Shawshank Redemption' where the inmate Brooks feeds a maggot to a crow hidden in his jacket. So the crew had to find a maggot that had died of natural causes before they could do the scene.

12. Generous guy! Keanu Reeves kept what he needed and gave away almost all his earnings from 'The Matrix'. He gave it to the special effects team, turning them all into millionaires. According to Reeves, "Money is the last thing I think about. I could live on what I have already made for the next few centuries".

13. To get the right ethereal affect for the spirits that get released

from the Ark at the climax of 'Raiders of the Last Ark', the crew filmed mannequins underwater in slow motion through a fuzzy lens.

14. Unforeseen dangers on set! While filming the crucifixion scene in 'Passion of the Christ', Jim Caviezel was actually struck by lightning.

15. A soldier's secret. Major Donnie Dunagan was the Marines' youngest-ever drill instructor. He served three tours in Vietnam, where he was wounded several times. But he never let anybody know he was also the voice of Disney's Bambi!

16. That's where he got his name! George Lucas' dog was named Indiana.

17. The total run time of 'Titanic' is the exact amount it took the actual Titanic to sink. And if you watch all 3 Saw films together, you will have spent 666 minutes doing so.

18. Graham Greene's character from 'Dances With Wolves' was meant to be a middle-aged man with bad posture. To ensure his awkward movements, he put a slice of slimy bologna in each of his shoes.

19. Taking a risk. During filming of 'Under The Skin', the men Scarlett Johansson's character lures into a van were not actors. Director Jonathan Glazer had cameras hidden inside to catch the real action, and only informed them afterwards that they were filming a movie.

20. Didn't break character! During filming of 'Django

Unchained', Leonardo DiCaprio slammed his hand onto a table and accidentally sliced it open on broken glass. He ignored it while the cameras rolled and continued on with the scene. It's the take they use in the film!

TEST YOURSELF - QUESTIONS AND ANSWERS

1. Nicolas Cage claims studying the movements of this pet helped him with his acting:

A) Octopus
B) Snake
C) Golden Retriever

2. Before becoming one of the most successful actors of all-time, Christopher Walken travelled with the circus as a:

A) Lion Tamer
B) Clown
C) Trapeze Artist

3. Harrison Ford was hanging a door for Francis Ford Coppola when he was asked to read for a role in which film?

A) Dead Heat on a Merry-Go-Round
B) American Graffiti
C) Star Wars

4. Stories of Japanese schoolgirls ambushing men who surfed the Internet to find underage dates inspired which film?

A) Hard Candy
B) An American Crime
C) The Girl Next Door

5. Most people know the first two rules of Fight Club. Which one is another from the list?

A) No showers before a fight

B) No kicking below the belt

C) Fights will go on as long as they have to.

ANSWERS

1. A
2. A
3. C
4. A
5. C

DON'T FORGET YOUR FREE BOOKS

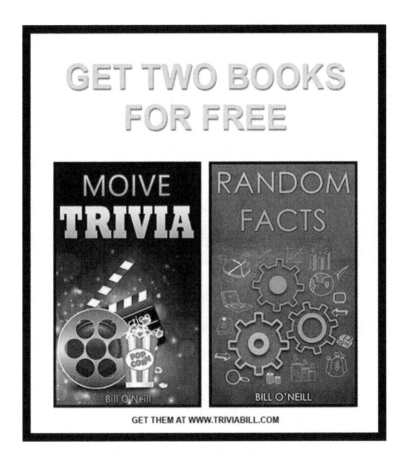

MORE BOOKS BY BILL O'NEILL

I hope you enjoyed this book and learned something new. Please feel free to check out some of my previous books on Amazon.